SEEING WITH THE HEART

How to Be Spiritual in an Unspiritual World

Rev. Dr. Johnnie William Skinner, Sr.

Foreword by
Dr. Gardner C. Taylor

Urban Ministries, Inc.
chicago, illinois

Publisher
Urban Ministries, Inc.
Chicago, Illinois
(312) 233-4499

First Edition
First Printing
ISBN: 0-940955-32-6
Catalog No. 9-6302

DEDICATION

This book is dedicated to the memory of
my brother Tom Skinner, whose life and ministry
inspired my vision and mission for the Church
and the African American community.

Johnnie William Skinner, Sr.

ACKNOWLEDGMENTS

I would like to acknowledge the following persons for their guidance and help in my spiritual journey. I thank my parents, the late Reverend Alester J. Skinner and Georgia Skinner, whose faith in the Lord and compassion for people made the difference in the direction of my life.

I would like to thank Reverend Stanley B. Long of the South Bay Community Church in California; Dr. William E. Pannell of Fuller Theological Seminary, Pasadena, California; and Reverend Dr. Samuel DeWitt Proctor, who served as my mentor at the United Theological Seminary in Dayton, Ohio. A special word of thanks to my pastor the Reverend Dr. Gardner Calvin Taylor for helping me to understand the importance of prayer in my life and ministry, and to the late Reverend Dr. M.L. Wilson of the Convent Avenue Baptist Church, New York City for the opportunity to serve in that church while a student at Union Theological Seminary in New York City.

Thank you, also to my friends in the ministry of Jesus Christ: the Reverends Calvin O. Butts, III, Charles S. Brown, Frederick C. Ennette, Daryl Ward, Ron Ballard, Joseph R. Hickman, Jr., Edward L. Wheeler, Margaret Mallory, Prathia Hall Wynn, Kevin M. Turman, Charles E. Booth, Charles A. McKinney, Lee Johnson and Mr. Christopher H. Woodhull.

My thanks and appreciation to my administrative assistant, Deborah S. Barnes for allowing the Lord to use her gifts for the English language in making possible the original work which served as the basis for this work. A word of thanks to Denise Gates, who served as the editor for this book.

··

I must thank the people of the Mount Zion Baptist Church of Knoxville, Tennessee for their prayerful support of this ministry.

A special word of thanks and appreciation to my spouse, Andrea, and my three sons: Johnnie, Calvin Taylor, and Thomas Corey for their love, support and patience.

I pray that this book will find meaning in the lives of those who read it. May the Lord of the Church receive all of the honor, glory, and praise.

TABLE OF CONTENTS

FOREWORD

Too long, too often, performance and prayer have been separated, attitude and action divorced. So! We have held the notion that if one is contemplative and prayerful, one cannot be assertive and active in the struggle for a better life.

This fine treatise seeks with resounding success to wipe out this dichotomy. If we had read the Gospel discerningly, we would have avoided this sad, and often fatal, separation. If we read the Gospel carefully we will discover that proper prayer produces performance, mandates it.

As we approach the climactic moments of our Lord's life, there is a brief but endlessly moving and instructive word about the joining of quiet, mystic communion to the noise and strife of life's great disputed passages, its momentous confrontations. At the end of the Last Supper, Matthew says they sang a hymn–contemplation, and went out into the great cosmic struggle with evil–crucifixion.

Johnnie Skinner, appropriately enough, summons us in this book to see and accept this union of worship and work, prayer and performance, contemplation and confrontation.

Dr. Gardner C. Taylor, Senior Pastor Emeritus
The Concord Baptist Church of Christ
Brooklyn, New York

PREFACE

The question of where God is in the African American religious experience is a very important one. The ancestors of African Americans were worshipers of the one God who was God of both the sacred and the secular. All activity was performed with a sense of the sacred in heart and in mind. For early African Americans, worship became so fully absorbed into the lives of the participants that it made the presence of God a reality under the worst of circumstances. It was this faith in the life, death, and resurrection power of the Redeemer that made it possible for an oppressed people to know God's power and empowerment in their lives.

There is no doubt that the African American worship experience has always been distinctive. The understanding that God is within all that people of African descent do is a vital part of our religious heritage. *Seeing With the Heart* examines the expression of spirituality in the African American Church experience as demonstrated through preaching, worship, and discipline. Within this context, the book discusses how spirituality is meant for both the interior and exterior life of today's African American Church.

Objectives. Upon completion of this book, the reader should be able to discuss how spirituality relates to the identity of both the believer and the Church. Questions such as who we are, why we exist, and what we want to do can be best answered with the understanding that God is in every area of our lives. Knowing our spiritual self-identity is essential to the fulfillment of the mission of the Church in this time. A goal of this book is to encourage the examination and discovery of who we are spiritually so that we

....

can become more effective in what we do as people of God.

Organization. This book is divided into 12 chapters. Chapter One provides an overall introduction and examines both historical and contemporary issues of spirituality. It defines the areas of preaching, worship, and discipline which serve as the context for exploring the African American worship experience.

Each chapter is based on a sermon given by the author, the Reverend Dr. Johnnie William Skinner, Sr., to his congregation at Mount Zion Baptist Church in Knoxville, Tennessee. The chapters are divided into three sections: an introduction, the sermon, and Bible Study Application. The Bible Study Application section contains three different sets of questions.

The questions allow the participants to examine what the Word of God has to say about the topic of each chapter. The Personal Ministry questions encourage the participants to look at their personal lives in light of the Word of God. Finally, the Church Ministry questions prompt participants to develop new ideas to improve the ministry of the Church.

Uses. This book can be used for both private and group study. It can be used in a variety of ways in the local church (training of teachers and deacons, Sunday School electives, Training Hour curriculum, weekday Bible studies, adult Vacation Bible School curriculum) and in family devotions.

Group Study—90-Minute Sessions. This book is designed for a two-part group study session. The participants should be encouraged to read each chapter in preparation for the sessions. In Part I of the session, participants examine the introduction to the chapter and the sermon that follows. Then the session leader divides the group into smaller groups to discuss the sermon in detail and answer the Bible Study Application questions. In the final group discussion, the participants reconvene with the larger group and report their findings.

Group Study—60-Minute Sessions. In shorter periods, it might be necessary to use part of the chapter as a stimulus for discussion during the group meeting itself. The other part of the chapter might be used as a "homework" assignment or for private devotional study.

Family Devotions. During the week preceding the study of a given chapter, each member would read the chapter privately and select a different question from the exercise for study. In devotions, the family would first discuss the introduction and sermon. Then each member would read the assigned question and present their opinion "round robin style." The family discussion could follow each question or be reserved until the end. The devotion should end with personal application and prayer.

Summary. This book can be used in a variety of ways. However, the main purpose is to encourage an increased spiritual awareness within the individual and to facilitate spiritual growth within the congregation.

I Seek Renewal

I seek the renewal of the spirit of my mind.

There is a spirit of mind without which it is impossible to discern truth. It is this set of mind that makes possible the experience of truth and distinguishes it from the experience of error. It is this spirit that recognizes or senses the false, the dishonest, the bogus thing. It is this attitude that determines the use to which facts are put.

This spirit of mind works in our behavior, in what we do, in what we say, whether our acts are strictly moral in character, or whether they have to do with the manner in which we deal with each other or the traffic of the market place or aught else. This spirit of mind is the factor upon which the integrity of performance rests.

Constantly, I must seek the renewal of the spirit of my mind, lest I become insensitive, dulled, unresponsive to the creative movement of the spirit of God with which life is instinct. True, the spirit of my mind is a gift from God but it must be ever held before Him for testing, for squaring.

Here in the quietness I seek the renewal of the spirit of my mind that I may be a living, vital instrument in His hands, this day!

I seek the renewal of the spirit of my mind. [1]

—Howard Thurman

•••••••••••••••••••• **CHAPTER ONE**

SPIRITUAL EXPLORATION

Have you ever been admonished, "Don't take the Scripture out of context"? Context is important. We need a frame of reference to understand the true meaning.

As we begin to discover and examine our spirituality, the same advice holds true. We must know who we are and where we have come from before we can determine where we are going and what our spirituality really means. Therefore, let us begin our spiritual journey by looking at the context.

The African American Worship Experience

John 4:23-24

Yet a time is coming and has now come when the true worshipers will worship the Father in spirit and in truth, for they are the kind of worshipers the Father seeks. God is spirit, and his worshipers must worship in spirit and in truth.

"African American," "Black," "Negro," "Colored"—all of these terms denote the separate, distinct style deemed characteristic of people of African descent. African American people understand to a large degree why churches are separated and segregated on Sunday mornings. It did not begin that way; it became that way because of a system of brutality and dehumanization. Although Africans accepted Christianity as their way of life, as slaves they were not permitted to be part of the Christian Church. So, they started their own churches and infused these churches with their own style of worship.

The distinctiveness of African American worship is understood best when we study the roots of the experience itself. African religious tradition was rooted in the concept of the entire self being involved. African people had a holistic view of existence. Like their African ancestors, African American worshipers understand the interrelatedness and interconnectedness of all things in life. Worship is not separate from the everyday struggles of life. In fact, the foundation of the worship experience is that God is involved in every area of our life.

The African American worshiper believes:

- God rules.
- God intervenes in the affairs of humankind.
- God understands our suffering and pain and is involved in the everyday world of people, especially people who are suffering.
- God through Jesus Christ, the Incarnate Word, suffers with people.
- God affirms the humanity of African American people, even in the midst of their trouble.

Worship also brings inspiration to the worshiper. Within the African American Christian tradition, the worship experience is the highlight of the week—the people of God coming together for the purpose of adoration, praise, preaching, and singing. "What a time, what a time!" Worship helps infuse the believer with a renewed strength and the courage to face another week of hardship or difficulty.

The worship experience is also an opportunity for an African American to express himself or herself as an individual. The worship experience is the setting in which everybody is somebody. There are no big "I's" and little "you's." The Church is the one place where everyone is a sister or brother and, for the older believers, a mother or father. It is the place where people are affirmed as human beings created in the image and likeness of God.

The freedom of fellowship, the sermons, the songs, the prayers, and the incandescent faith that God will vindicate them in the end are the ingredients that make up the spiritual life of African American people. This spirituality is what makes the African American worship experience wonderfully distinctive.

Elements of Worship

The African American worship experience consists of three basic elements: music, prayer, and preaching.

Music

Music has always been an integral part of African worship. In a similar manner, the spirituals were at the root of the African American worship experience. The spiritual music of African American people did not come out of a tradition of power, position, or privilege. Under the whip of the slave master, hundreds of songs were forged in suffering. Slaves sang out of their experience, not from some esoteric understanding of the nature of God. The songs of slaves helped both the singer and the hearer achieve a better understanding of who God was in the midst of this brutal existence. They wanted God to be real for them in the midst of their pain. They knew that even if they could not speak, they could sing. They could "... sing the Lord's song in a strange land" (Psalm 137:4, paraphrased). The music captured the slaves' longing to be free.

The hundreds of spirituals forged out of the inhumanity of slavery indicate the remarkable resilience of our ancestors in the face of great and grave difficulty. The songs that developed out of the slaves' experiences were part and parcel of their own sense of God's presence; hence, they were able to sing, "Nobody knows the trouble I've seen—glory, hallelujah." In spite of their adversities and difficulties, they understood that God was present with them.

Needless to say, Africans did not study European music until much later. Because of our African heritage, African American worship involves the rhythm of dance and music. "African people had to adapt their African traditions towards Christianity; [it was] not that Blacks took Euro-Christian patterns and changed them towards their own needs. The root continuum is African."[2] Thus, to denigrate the way in which some African Americans sing or shout is to cast aspersions upon the source (the root cause and condition) of such actions.

The humanity of African Americans is affirmed through music. The kinds of songs chosen, even those that are not spirituals, have a quality of affirmation about them. For instance, Isaac Watts' hymn, "Amazing Grace," has been adopted by African Americans through the years as a theme song of God's grace. Of the various arrangements, the one most characteristic of the African American Christian Church is one-lined out in a common-meter arrangement: someone, usually a deacon, would call out the lines of the hymn, and then the congregation, in a slow, metered response, would repeat the lines in a chorus. The words to "Amazing Grace" have offered hope to many generations of worshipers.

> Through many dangers toils and snares
>
> I have already come;
>
> 'Tis grace that brought me safe thus far,
>
> And grace will lead me home.[3]

How important it is for the music of the worship experience to ring out in the hearts of believers.

African American music uplifts and inspires the worshipers to find release and relief from the everyday pressures and stresses of life. It creates an atmosphere that makes it easier for prayers to be uttered and the message of the sermon to be heard. Like the prayers and the preaching, the songs of the Church also help us understand the work and will of God.

Prayer

Prayer is communication with Almighty God. Our African American forebears prayed in the cabins, in the fields, and in the master's house. Their prayers were uttered with the knowledge that God is not only transcendent but also imminent. God is out there as well as here. They prayed for freedom, for justice, for an end to the brutality of slavery and oppression.

Prayer was liberating. It was not just the language or the words of prayer, it was the "worth of prayer" that had meaning and depth in their lives. Prayer means waiting before God. It involves waiting for God to answer, waiting for God to act in some way, or waiting for God to make a way, somehow. The spirituality of the African American means having a "patient endurance" before the throne of God. "They that wait upon the Lord shall renew their strength...." (Isaiah 40:31, KJV). Prayer is understood as being an activity; prayer is active, not passive. Waiting takes on a new form when you are waiting upon the Lord. Prayer is what Jesus meant when He said, "Watch and pray" (Matthew 26:41, KJV).

The prayers of the African American worshiper are also an affirmation of our humanity before the living God. Prayers affirm who we are and what we can be. For African American worshipers to be able to come before God means that they are people, too. "I am somebody," the worshiper can proclaim within his or her own heart and mind. We are part of the kingdom of priests, a royal nation, chosen of God. The African American worshiper can clearly declare, "We are God's children, too."

Prayer meetings are a special time in the life of the African American Christian Church. Traditionally held on Wednesday evening, the prayer meeting usually brings the people of God together in a warmer, more intimate setting than is characteristic of Sunday morning worship. During the prayer meeting, old hymns are more likely to be sung, testimonies can be uttered, and people can pray "without form or fashion."

Some may ask, "Why all this emphasis on prayer? What do prayers accomplish? How can prayer change the lives or circumstances of those who pray?" Prayer is more than words; it is also a way of communicating the deepest needs and desires of the heart before a loving and merciful God who hears and answers prayer. This is the basic belief of all those who pray. The one who prays comes before God with a sense of awe and a sense of God's majesty and power. Prayer is a privilege granted by God because of the work of redemption through Jesus Christ. Prayer invites the living God to intervene in the life of the believer. In the book *Religious Living*,[4] Georgia Harkness states seven principles of prayer:

- Prayer must be centered on God.
- Prayer must be natural.
- Prayer must be unrehearsed.
- Prayer must be intellectually sincere.
- Prayer must combine alertness with passivity.
- Prayer must be accompanied by active effort.
- Prayer must be based on intelligent trust.

African American Christians understand that they cannot make it through life without prayer, no matter what level of educational attainment (Ph.D. to No.D.) or status in the community they might possess. God's people will pray. A true sense of spirituality is developed in an atmosphere of prayer.

Preaching

Spirituality is mediated through the preaching and application of the Word of God, the Bible. The sermons which the slaves preached and heard reveal the lasting endurance of the Word in the life of a believer. The Bible, which was used by slave masters in many instances to make their slaves docile and obedient, later became the Book that would chart the course of liberation for the enslaved community. The sermon became the instrument through which the slave preacher could communicate—often in a kind of coded language understood only by the flock—the message of freedom and hope. For instance, when telling the story of how Moses was called out and used as God's messenger, the slave preacher could emphasize that God said, "Tell ol' Pharaoh to let my people go." The sermon planted into the hearts and minds of the hearers the truth that there is freedom in Jesus Christ. It then became possible for the slaves to envision and anticipate a new future—one without the shackles of slavery and the whip of the slave master.

The African American Christian worship service is arranged so as to move worshipers toward the hearing of the Word. There must be a sense that when people come together they will hear a word from the Lord. The preaching of the Word is the centerpiece of the African American worship experience. Without the Word, the worship experience would lack the power, force, and authority needed to motivate and enable those worshiping. Through the Spirit of God, the Word brings healing, conviction, and deliverance. It also calls the people to faith, repentance, and to greater service in the name of the risen Lord.

Preaching is the empowering event of the worship service. We are reminded of the Scripture that states, "But how are men [and women] to call upon Him in whom they have not believed? And how are they to believe in Him whom they have not heard? And how are they to hear without a preacher? And how can the preacher preach unless he or she is sent.... For faith comes by hearing, and hearing by the word of God" (Romans 10:14-15, 17, NRSV). It is often said that the people will forgive a preacher for almost anything except not being able to preach.

Through the homiletical tradition of the African American Church, the sermon should create a desire to know more about the Lord and the experience of being almost overwhelmed, as it were, by the presence of the Holy Spirit. The sermon points the worshiper in the direction of the Eternal. It describes what it means to have a vital relationship with the living God and sensitizes its hearers to the needs of those around them. The sermon seeks to unravel the mystery of spirituality by explaining how we may enter into that "mystic union" in Christ Jesus.

The sermon must also speak to the needs of the people. People want information as well as inspiration. A good sermon will help the worshiper throughout the week by addressing both the spiritual and societal realities of the hearer. Some of the hearers will already have some understanding of how God is at work in the circumstances of their lives. Others may have come wondering whether God is working at all. The sermon should be reassuring for the former group and informative for the latter. The Lord says, "Do not fear, for I am with you; do not be afraid, for I am your God. I will strengthen you; I will help you; I will uphold you with my victorious right hand" (Isaiah 41:10, NRSV). This, then, is the aim of the sermon—to let people know that in spite of or because of life and its circumstances, God is with them.

Spiritual Discipline

Even as slaves, the forbearers of the present-day African American Church understood that a spiritual foundation had to be laid in order for future generations to achieve freedom, dignity, and equality.

"Spirituality" is the term used to describe the abiding presence of the Holy Spirit in both the inner life of the believer and the atmosphere of the worship experience. It is the presence of the Holy Spirit that moves believers toward a deeper communion with God and affects their relationships with others. The activity of the Holy Spirit in the life of the Church compels every believer to reach out to meet the needs of others and to worship God in spirit and in truth.

Spirituality is more than some nebulous notion about Black people and their relationship with God; it also works itself out in some very concrete ways. These concrete ways have to do with the personal, social, and political issues that affect the lives of Black people every day.

Spirituality in the African American Church experience means discipline of the heart and the mind. It requires the total commitment of one's being to the power and presence of the Holy Spirit. "Thou shalt love the Lord thy God with all thy heart, and with all thy soul, and with all thy mind" (Matthew 22:37, KJV). Our hearts and minds are involved so that the presence of God may become more real to us each day. Because of our roots in African traditional religion, an expected and accepted manifestation of the Holy Spirit's presence in the worship service is evidenced by the shout. However, the presence of the Holy Spirit in everyday life does not result in uncontrolled emotional behavior. The Holy Spirit brings discipline into the life of the believer. The Holy Spirit sensitizes the individual to an awareness of the need for growth.

Evidence of Spiritual Growth

Spiritual growth includes the development of "holy habits" which keep us open to the presence of God. These are simple habits, such as Bible reading, private and public prayer, worship, and fellowship with other believers. Good spiritual health is analogous to a good physical regimen. One must eat properly, exercise, and rest in order to stay in good physical condition. So it is with our spiritual lives. There must be spiritual exercise, as well as the intake of the kind of spiritual ingredients into our lives that will keep us spiritually fit.

Our spiritual health is not just for our benefit; it is also for the benefit of the believing community and beyond. Our spirituality cannot ignore the social realities of our times. Gayraud Wilmore states,

"My thesis is that what we call the black religious tradition nurtures and promotes both spirituality and militancy for social change in varying and complex ways."

He goes on to say,

"Spirituality and social transformation are not only two sides of the same coin, but are also so interpenetrated that the black religionist cannot rest without both."[5]

It is important for the Church to be cognizant of its relationship to society. Spirituality means being political. Spirituality calls us to involvement in the world. Spirituality denotes a relationship with the Spirit, but it does not dismiss the material or physical world. It is through a renewal of our spirituality that we are further sensitized to the needs of people around us.

To be God's people in the world certainly means that we must take a stand on the issues of our day. In order for us to confront these issues, our spiritual preparedness must be ever before us. Spirituality implies dramatic and radical transformation, and inward and outward change. Courts, state legislatures, and Congress all have a part in changing the direction of people's behavior. However, spiritual transformation goes to the very core of the human dilemma. This is not to suggest that we adopt the "wait 'til Jesus comes" attitude that even the fundamentalists of our times have apparently abandoned. We need to allow ourselves to be renewed as the courageous and creative people of God in the presence of the Holy Spirit. The Holy Spirit will energize and empower us to meet the tasks we face.

The African American Church has been in the forefront of dramatic social change in recent history. This desire for social change has its basis in the understanding that God can and does change human lives and human situations. Change begins in the worship service and in the prayer meeting. Real and lasting change is only possible when people have been changed through the power of the Holy Spirit.

Spiritual Direction

Each new generation of the Christian Church seeks to define its own mission. Central to any understanding or statement of mission in the Christian Church is the need to define and understand the concept of spirituality. Discovering a spiritual self-identity is essential to fulfillment of the mission of the Church in our time. Once we discover a sense of spirituality, the other matters will become clearer to us—especially matters concerning our involvement in the social reality of this generation. Spiritual and social realities are part of the same basic reality. However, it is only when we discover who we are that we can become effective in reaching humanity.

The African American Church has a glorious past and

untapped potential to do a greater good in both the local community and the world. The future lies before us to make a difference in the lives of the people in the congregation, so as to equip them to go forth and make an equally significant difference in the community, as well. However, the Church can only be as good or effective as its sense of spirituality and the extent to which that spirituality is developed and exercised.

For African Americans, the context in which our new spirituality is developed is not that new after all. Our discovery and venture into faith is deeply rooted in a past charged with the spirituality of a people who knew and loved the Lord. They were a people who knew how to let go of everything but God. Slaves, but they looked to a heavenly Master; locked out, but not kept out by society's harsh laws; ignored, but insistent that God was (and is) just and rules with a hand of power and love. The foundation has been laid for us to continue to face the future in faith, empowered by the indwelling presence of God's Holy Spirit.

Facing the Future

As we move toward the 21st century, spirituality must take on a new significance for the African American Church. If the African American Christian Church is going to have a significant impact on people, then the work of the Holy Spirit must be demonstrated in the life of the Church; people must be able to see God at work. People need to know that the Church does have a vital and viable relationship with Jesus Christ and that the people of God are sensitive to the needs of the people around them. When people in a given community begin to see the people of God in action, then the community is enabled to respond in a positive way to the Gospel of Jesus Christ.

27

There are risks involved in this new spiritual exploration. The risk of giving up accepted traditions and stepping out into uncharted territory—embracing new forms of spiritual development. Other possible risks might include undertaking new forms of worship and/or reconstructing the organizational character of the Church in order to meet the needs of the people more directly. In spite of these risks, however, there are also limitless possibilities in terms of what can be done to make the Church move forward spiritually.

With a new sense of spiritual direction, with a new mission and ministry, the present-day African American Christian Church will be able to step out to fulfill its mission of "making disciples" for Christ. We have just started; we have a long way to go. Nevertheless, with the continuing abiding presence of the Holy Spirit, we will be able to do the work God has given our hearts and hands to do.

BIBLE STUDY APPLICATION

Who Are We?
(Defining Church, Spirituality, Worship, and Discipline)

When we think of the Church, of what do we think? Do we think of an institution, a social organization, a social club, a political organization, or an economic order? What images of the Church are conjured in our minds? Thoughts of revival services, Sunday School, BTU, BYF, or various other activities that over the years have meant church. For many, church is one of the activities on a list of "things to do today." Often, people outside the church could care less about what we do inside. In many circles, the church is seen as being irrelevant and archaic. How should we define the Church? Let's begin by looking to see what the Word of God has to say.

Using the Scripture verses as a foundation for your answers, describe how the Bible defines or explains the following terms.

1. What is the Church?
   (Ephesians 5:23; Colossians 1:18; Romans 12:5; 1 Corinthians 3:23; 7:23; 12:27)

2. Why does the Church exist?
   (Isaiah 43:7; Romans 11:36; Ephesians 3:21; 1 Corinthians 6:19-20; Revelation 4:11; 5:12-13)

3. Why is the worship experience important?
   (Exodus 34:14; 2 Kings 17:36-39; Psalm 95:3-7; John 4:22-24)

4. Describe the role of music in the African American worship experience.
   (1 Chronicles 15:16; 2 Chronicles 5:13; Psalm 95:1-2; 144:9; 150:4; Ephesians 5:19; Colossians 3:16; Hebrews 2:12)

5. Describe the role of prayer in the African American worship experience.
   (Psalm 66:20; 102:1-2; Proverbs 15:29; Matthew 6:6-13; 21:22; John 14:13-14; Philippians 4:6; Hebrews 4:14-16; James 5:15-16)

6. Describe the role of the sermon in the African American worship experience.

(Psalm 107:20; John 8:32; Romans 10:8-17; 1 Corinthians 1:18, 21; 2 Corinthians 4:5-7; Ephesians 5:26-27; Hebrews 4:12)

7. What is spirituality?
(John 14:17; Acts 1:8; 4:31; Romans 8:9, 15-16; 1 Corinthians 3:16; 2 Timothy 1:7; 1 John 2:27; 3:24; 4:13)

8. What is spiritual discipline?
(Ecclesiastes 12:13-14; Isaiah 58:6; Psalm 119:9, 11; Proverbs 23:12; Matthew 5:16; John 14:21; 1 Corinthians 10:31; 15:58; 2 Timothy 2:15; James 1:22; 1 John 3:18)

Where Do We Come From?
(Is History Really Important?)

From its inception, the African American Christian Church has been on a journey of faith. From the very beginning, the African American believer possessed an indomitable spirit which held on to the vision of a better tomorrow until the reality of a new day of freedom dawned. Even in the midst of civil strife and unrest in this country, the African American Church continued to seek out and act on its mission as the people of God.

9. Why is the expression of spirituality within the African American Christian Church distinctive?

10. Describe how earlier traditions affect the music, prayer, and preaching of today's worship experience.
11. Discuss the legacy of leadership that brought the African American Church to this place and time.

What Are We to Do?

(Whose Job Is It? Defining Roles and Responsibilities)

To our dismay, some African American churches of today are becoming increasingly distant from the mainstream of the African American community. In today's economy, many churches have been forced to turn their focus toward making mortgage payments. Oftentimes, due to the need to make these payments, the church becomes unable to develop significant ministries that would take its members beyond its doors. God's people must begin to sense and act on the belief that now is the time to move away from a mortgage mentality to ministry development, both internally and externally.

The Church must become spiritually prepared to do what God has called us to do in the future. The pastors and people of generations past have brought us to this moment and we cannot allow it to pass us by. The need is great, and we have the Source and resources available to us to do God's will.

12. Identify the challenges of meeting the physical needs of a diverse population. Discuss the similarity of human spiritual needs.
    (John 3:16; Acts 4:12; Romans 3:23; 5:8; Philippians 4:19; 1 Timothy 2:5; Hebrews 4:16)

13. What is the role of the African American Church?
    (Matthew 5:13; 9:37-38; 28:19-20; Luke 10:2; John 15:5; Acts 1:8; 1 Corinthians 3:9; 12:27; Galatians 3:26-28; 1 Thessalonians 5:5; 1 Peter 2:9; 1 John 2:14; 3:18; 4:4)

14. Discuss the importance of the vision or mission of the Church.
    (Proverbs 29:18)

CHURCH MINISTRY APPLICATION

Review and discuss your church's mission statement or statement of faith.

1. Describe the vision and direction of the local church. (Habakkuk 2:2)

2. Identify the plan or method of realizing the vision. (Matthew 5:16)

3. Describe the "price of involvement" and the benefits of pursuing the local church's vision and mission. (Luke 14:28; Hebrews 11:6)

If Thou Standeth Beside Me

If Thou standeth beside me
Nothing can prevail against me.

"If THOU standeth beside me." There are times when the sense of aloneness is very acute. Often these are times of struggle where the odds are uneven. Curious indeed is it that the sense of not being alone is apt to be most acutely felt when the concentration upon the matter at hand is absorbing. This means that there is available, at the moment, no margin of me exposed to the Presence of God. To be aware that God is standing beside me calls for some measure of detachment from my own personal struggle and turmoil.

"If Thou standeth beside me." It is entirely possible that the Presence of God may be most acutely felt in and through the struggle and the turmoil. It is not something apart from my involvements but a quality of Presence that emerges from the midst of my tempests. Or more accurately, it becomes a quality of the tempest itself. Sometimes this identification becomes very confusing, causing me to say that God brings the struggle. It is sufficient for me to know that He is found in the midst of all that befalls me. Nothing can prevail against me. The affirmation is the result of the disclosure of the Presence of God in the midst of what befalls me. First, He is felt as being with, in and among the struggling elements of my experience. Then, out of the midst of these, His presence emerges and becomes One who stands by my side. It is then that I am lifted up and strengthened.

If Thou standeth beside me
Nothing can prevail against me.[6]

—*Howard Thurman*

THE TRIALS OF LIFE

It is difficult being a Christian, particularly in these times. The adversary of our souls seems to be on the offensive all around us. No one is immune to the onslaught of the enemy. The burglar is tempted to steal from the bank; the drug addict is tempted to take more drugs. The politician is tempted to overlook the needs of the people for his or her own interest. Temptations come in various forms to lure us into the trap. It is like the con games, scams—the old shell games, the old card tricks which are played on people every day.

Sometimes we are caught between the proverbial rock and a hard place on this journey. We must deal with our inner weaknesses and negative desires. Temptations are common to all of us; no one escapes. We are all tempted to be less than we want to be—even Jesus suffered temptation. However, there is good news for us. We can win the victory in the battle between the good and evil impulses in our lives and overcome the trials and tests of life.

The War in the Wilderness

Matthew 4:1-11

Then Jesus was led by the Spirit into the desert to be tempted by the devil. After fasting forty days and forty nights, he was hungry. The tempter came to him and said, "If you are the Son of God, tell these stones to become bread."

Jesus answered, "It is written: 'Man does not live on bread alone, but on every word that comes from the mouth of God.'

Then the devil took him to the holy city and had him stand on the highest point of the temple. "If you are the Son of God," he said, "throw yourself down. For it is written:

"'He will command his angels concerning you,
and they will lift you up in their hands,
so that you will not strike your foot against
a stone.'"

Jesus answered him, "It is also written: 'Do not put the Lord your God to the test.'"

Again, the devil took him to a very high mountain and showed him all the kingdoms of the world and their splendor. "All this I will give you," he said, "if you will bow down and worship me."

Jesus said to him, "Away from me, Satan! For it is written: 'Worship the Lord your God, and serve him only.'"

Then the devil left him, and angels came and attended him.

After the baptism of Jesus, the Holy Spirit led Him into the wilderness to be tempted. Upon reading this, I thought, "Why would the Spirit of God lead Jesus into the wilderness?" The answer is clear. If Jesus came to die for our sins, and if He was to understand our conditions, He would need to understand our testings and trials. Jesus had to face temptation in order to help us.

Our Lord came to earth to fulfill His mission as the Son of God; the Word became flesh and dwelt among us (John 1:14). Jesus was born without sin. The enemy had to tempt Jesus because there was no sin in Him. The Bible says that He was in all points tempted as we are, yet without sin (Hebrews 4:15). It becomes evident, then, that if all of us suffer temptations, so must Jesus. The temptations which Jesus faced represent the temptations we face in our own lives.

Temptation #1: Satisfaction

We are tempted to put the emphasis on the wrong areas of our lives. Martin Luther King, Jr., said, "We major in the minors and minor in the majors." The first temptation was an appeal to the basic biophysical needs in Jesus and in all of us. The tempter appeals to Jesus' hunger, because He had fasted 40 days and 40 nights. The tempter will always appeal to our fleshly needs.

The temptation to turn stones into bread (Matthew 4:3) also represents the temptation to make more out of what we have. The success of our lives is often gauged by the jobs we have, the homes in which we live, and the cars we drive. There is something in us which hungers for the things of this world. The tempter appeals to the hunger of our hearts.

There is a real hunger in all of us, but counterfeit nutrition will not fill it. There is a need in us to find satisfaction, joy, and peace of mind in our own world. Our hunger is deeper than this world's resources can meet. This is the trick of the adversary: he would like us to think that we are capable of meeting our own needs. The tempter knows that we really don't know what we really need. Thus, he knows that we will try anything to satisfy the hunger in us.

We try it all—from alcohol to treachery. We indulge in everything we can find to answer our hunger. "Turn these stones into bread; get rich quick; sell drugs; wield power, step on people; meet your deepest need for fun"—all of these enticements relate to one another. "Try this, and you will find satisfaction," says the tempter. Jesus replies by saying, "Man shall not live by bread alone, but by every word that proceeds from the mouth of God" (4:4, RSV).

Our need is spiritual and we cannot rely upon what we see, touch, and smell to meet that need. There is the story of the group of babies somewhere in Central or South America who had been getting all of the physical nourishment they needed; however, they were still ill and failed to thrive. Some of them were dying. They discovered that because these children were not receiving enough affection and love, they were suffering. Love is spiritual. Enough food, but not enough care; enough physical nourishment, but not enough love. Our most important basic needs are spiritual.

Temptation #2: Suicide

The next temptation was the temptation toward senseless direction and hopelessness. Satan asks Jesus to jump from the pinnacle of the temple. Sometimes the devil tempts us to risk losing our spiritual lives. The test of our faith in God is often taken to the extreme. It becomes almost absurd: "Jump down and the angels will bear you up." In other words, "Commit spiritual suicide," we are told. "Go without knowing where you are going. Go with the wrong crowd; it doesn't matter. Get in the car with the drunk, or crack head, or doped-up driver. What difference will it make? It's all right; you'll be okay—you're young, you know. You know the Scripture that says, 'God takes care of fools and babies.' Just jump, and God will look after you."

Remember that the devil is the father of lies (John 8:44). As we trust God and obey God's holy will, God will take care of us. God is the giver of life, and we are to guard the gift. Do not test or tempt the Lord your God.

Temptation #3: Success and Power

The next temptation was the offer of political, social, and economic power. "Look at what I can give you, if you will bow down and worship me," the devil said (Matthew 4:9, paraphrased). Power is often understood as control or domination of others—the authority to command or control the lives of other people. There are those who will come to you and say, "I will do this for you, if you worship me. Sell your soul to me; sell your self-respect; sell your honor; sell your dignity, and I will give you the world. I will give you prestige, power, privilege, and position." These are all forms of power, but at what price?

As Lord Acton said, "Power corrupts, and absolute power corrupts absolutely." Power does not come without a price, and often the price is very high indeed. "Fall down and worship me," the devil says to us. "Kowtow, if you will; give up your soul, if you will." In Mark 8:36, Jesus asked, "What does it profit a person, if he or she gains the whole world but loses his or her own soul?"

My sisters and brothers, there is only one to whom we owe our loyalty, allegiance, and love and that is Jesus Christ. He is our Saviour, our Deliverer, and our Healer.

Jesus tells Satan, "Get away from me. It is written, 'Worship the Lord your God and only Him will you serve'" (Matthew 4:10). God judges, directs, leads, and blesses. We need the Lord to help, and only God can help us.

After the Testing

After the temptations, Satan leaves and the angels come and attend to the needs of Jesus Christ (4:11). The trial of Jesus exhausted Him. In facing the stresses and strains of life, we will often come out spiritually and emotionally exhausted. We will need the support of ministering angels who will come in the form of persons who understand what we are going through and will offer a word of encouragement, a word of comfort, or a word of prayer on our behalf. In Hebrews 2:18, the Bible states that Jesus Himself will minister to us. Because Jesus was tempted, He is able to help us. He is able to empower us to meet the critical challenges we face in our neighborhoods, communities, and the world. He is able to deliver us from the temptations that seek to destroy our lives.

Unlike worldly power, spiritual empowerment means being able to give oneself to God in service and to help others to do God's will. Spiritual power comes from spiritual growth and development. In order to develop spiritually, we must face struggle. The axiom "no pain, no gain" is as true as the saying "no cross, no crown." Our spirituality is developed in the trials and temptations of this present life. The abiding presence of God's Holy Spirit makes us overcomers, and strengthens us to do what God has called us to do and to become what God has called us to be.

Winning the War

How do we win the war in the wilderness? We will win the war in the wilderness when we recognize that our need is spiritual, not just physical. We are often tempted by the "things" of this world, which we are encouraged to believe will satisfy our needs. The basic need of our lives, however, is spiritual. St. Augustine is believed to have expressed this need thusly, "Our souls will not rest until they find rest in Thee, O God." The bread of this world will not satisfy us for long. Only the bread of heaven can do that.

We will win the war when we recognize that God's love is everlasting and unyielding, but God must not be tempted. Our trust in God must be constant, not sensational. Trust in God means that we depend on the promises of God to sustain us in our times of trial and temptation. We must believe the Word and trust in God always, not just in the face of some dramatic occurrence.

We must recognize that to win the war in the wilderness, the glory belongs to God and not to us. The glory and glamour of this world last but a fleeting moment; but only what is done for Christ will last (1 Corinthians 3:12). The Scriptures say, "...we look not at what can be seen, but at what cannot be seen: for what can be seen is temporary; but what cannot be seen is eternal" (2 Corinthians 4:18, NRSV).

The war goes on in every aspect of our lives, but the victory is ours with God, for "...we are more than conquerors through Him that loved us" (Romans 8:37, NRSV).

BIBLE STUDY APPLICATION

Passing the Tests of Life

Tests come in various forms. Just as Jesus had to face and overcome trials and temptations in His life, so do we. Our challenge is to meet any attempt to weaken our spirituality in the power of the Holy Spirit.

1. Temptations are common to all of us; no one escapes. What does God promise to do for us when we confront temptation? (1 Corinthians 10:13)

2. Why was Jesus tempted? (Hebrews 2:17-18, 4:15)

3. There is a real hunger in all of us. We often try to fulfill spiritual needs with physical things. What does the Bible say that we are tempted by? (James 1:13-14)

4. The world will also offer temptations to lure us from our faith in Jesus Christ. What types of satisfaction does the world offer us? (1 John 2:16)

5. The temptations which Jesus faced represent the temptations we face in our own lives. Read the account in Luke 4:1-14 of Jesus' temptation in the wilderness.
   a) In Luke 4:4, what was Jesus' response to the temptation to satisfy the lust of the flesh (gaining food)?
   b) What was His response to that same kind of temptation in John 4:34?
   c) In Luke 4:8, what was Jesus' response to the temptation to satisfy the lust of the eyes (gaining the kingdoms of the world)?

d) What was His response to that same kind of temptation in John 18:36?

e) In Luke 4:12, what was Jesus' response to the temptation to satisfy the pride of life (exercising His authority over the angels)?

f) What was His response to that same kind of temptation in John 6:38?

g) What was His response to the temptation to walk in darkness or hopelessness in John 8:12?

h) In Luke 4:14, how did Jesus leave the encounter in the wilderness to begin His public ministry?

6. We will overcome temptation when we recognize that our most important needs are spiritual.

a) What does Jesus say about gaining spiritual food? (John 4:10-14; 6:35; 7:37-38; Matthew 5:6)

b) What does Jesus say about gaining the kingdom of God? (Matthew 6:33; John 3:3)

c) What does the Bible say about gaining spiritual authority? (Matthew 18:4; 23:12; Philippians 2:5-11)

Victory Over Temptation

The war has been won. Jesus won the victory at the Cross; the devil was defeated. However, we are called to walk in victory as overcomers in this life. Jesus overcame the devil by using the same weapons that are available to us today: the Word of God ("It is written"), the power of the Spirit (Mark 1:10; Luke 4:1, 14), and prayer (Luke 3:21; 22:40, 46).

....

7. How does the Bible describe the battle against the devil? (John 16:33; Romans 12:21; 1 Corinthians 15:57; 2 Corinthians 2:14; 10:3-5; Ephesians 6:10-12; Hebrews 2:14-15; James 4:7; 1 John 3:8; 4:4; 5:4-5)

8. To be overcomers, we must know how to use our weapons. Look up the following Scriptures to see how the Bible describes these weapons.
   a) The Word of God (Ephesians 6:17; Hebrews 4:12)
   b) The power of the Holy Spirit (John 16:13; Acts 1:8; Romans 15:13, 19; 1 Corinthians 12:3)
   c) Prayer (Philippians 4:6-7; James 5:15-16)

9. What does the Bible say about overcoming the desires of the flesh? (Romans 8:12-13; 13:14; Galatians 3:3; 5:16-17, 24; 1 Peter 4:1-2)

10. What does the Bible say about overcoming the desires of the mind? (Matthew 22:37; Romans 8:6; 12:2; 1 Corinthians 3:18-21; Philippians 2:5-11; 2 Timothy 1:7)

11. What rewards are promised to those who overcome? (James 1:12; Revelation 2:7, 11, 17, 26; 3:5, 12, 21; 21:7)

PERSONAL APPLICATION

1. Check yourself. Are there areas in your life where you are willing to give up character, honor, dignity, or self-respect to gain the rewards of this world?

SEEING WITH THE HEART

2. If the government took away your name, social security number, address, and job title, who would you be?

3. What is the most difficult temptation that you are facing today?

4. In light of this sermon, how would you define the following:
   a) True satisfaction
   b) Tempting the Lord
   c) The price of power

5. In Luke 9:23, why do you think Jesus asks His followers to deny themselves, take up their cross daily, and follow Him?

CHURCH MINISTRY APPLICATION

1. What should be our response when we see others fighting temptation?

2. Before Jesus went out into public ministry, He won private victory over temptation. Describe the value of a personal testimony in showing others that the Holy Spirit provides real power over temptation.

3. Consider how the Church can become more effective in equipping the congregation to fight and win today's battle.

The Outer Life and the Inward Sanctuary

*I determine to live the outer life
in the inward sanctuary.*

Often it is very hard for me to realize that I am one. The outer life seems utterly outer. It seems a part of a separate order. It is made up of the things I do, of my relationships of one kind or another with work, play, job, people and things. The standard by which the outer is judged tends to be an artificial standard, made up of that which is convenient, practical, expedient. The outer seems public, it seems ever to be an external net of physical relationships.

The inward sanctuary is my sanctuary. It is the place where I keep my trust with all my meaning and my values. It is the quiet place where the ultimate issues of my life are determined. What I know of myself, my meaning; what I know of God, His meaning; all this, and much more is made clear in my secret place. It seems strangely incongruous, often to bring into my secret place the rasping, gritty noises of my outer life. Again, this may be for me merely an alibi. For I know that in the searching light of my inward sanctuary all the faults, limitations and evil of my outer life stand clearly revealed for what they are.

I determine to live the outer life in the inward sanctuary. The outer life must find its meaning, the source of its strength in the inward sanctuary. As this is done, the gulf between outer and inner will narrow, and my life will be increasingly whole and of one piece. What I do in the outer will be blessed by the holiness of the inward sanctuary.

I determine to live the outer life in the inward sanctuary.[7]

—Howard Thurman

CHAPTER THREE

HIDDEN
IN CHRIST

She looked the same, but she knew that from this day on her life would change. She was an expectant mother. It was almost hard to believe that she carried a little baby inside of her—a new life that depended upon her for his or her survival. She determined that with God's help she would do all she could to take care of herself and her baby until the time for delivery.

Just as a baby is hidden inside the womb of its mother, to find the fullness of Christian living, we must allow ourselves to be hidden in Christ. What does it mean to be "in Christ"?

Someone has called the Christian life not only a changed life but also an exchanged life. As we surrender our lives to God, in exchange we receive the life of Christ. Identification with Christ in the crucifixion means that the believer's life is hidden with Christ in God (Colossians 3:3). Being one with Christ gives us the freedom and the power to be and do all that God has called us to be in our daily living.

The Lost "I"

Galatians 2:15-21

*"We who are Jews by birth and not 'Gentile sinners'
know that a man is not justified by observing the law, but
by faith in Jesus Christ. So we, too, have put our faith in
Christ Jesus that we may be justified by faith in Christ and
not by observing the law, because by observing the law no
one will be justified.*

*"If, while we seek to be justified in Christ, it becomes
evident that we ourselves are sinners, does that mean that
Christ promotes sin? Absolutely not! If I rebuild what I
destroyed, I prove that I am a lawbreaker. For through the
law I died to the law so that I might live for God. I have
been crucified with Christ and I no longer live, but Christ
lives in me. The life I live in the body, I live by faith in the
Son of God, who loved me and gave himself for me. I do
not set aside the grace of God, for if righteousness could
be gained through the law, Christ died for nothing!"*

Spirituality demands that we respond in some significant way to Christ's claims upon our lives. What does
Christ demand? The Book of Galatians, which is considered by many to be the "Magna Carta" for Christians, sets
forth the claim of our freedom in Christ. In Galatians, the
Apostle Paul emphasizes the believer's identification with
Christ and His death. Paul sets the tone for our liberation
from the works of the Law and establishes the truth of our
new relationship in Jesus Christ.

For the Christian to have a full understanding of his or her relationship in Jesus, the believer must recognize that justification comes through faith in Jesus Christ and not by the works of the Law. Salvation begins and ends in Jesus Christ. The Law only exposes one's sinfulness and weaknesses. The Law could not give life, it could only condemn. The person who keeps the Law cannot be saved by it, only judged by it. Paul proclaims in Romans, and affirms in Galatians, that the just shall live by faith—faith in Jesus Christ.

Christians often have a hard time changing from trust in their older traditions to complete trust in Jesus Christ. The Bible clearly states that no one can work his or her way into heaven. Salvation is a gift from God—given in response to a person's faith in the suffering, death, and resurrection of Jesus Christ (Ephesians 2:8-9). Our faith in who Christ is and what He has done for us produces a new spiritual relationship that liberates us from the works of the Law and the traditions of people.

As we are baptized into Jesus Christ, we are raised in the newness of life (Romans 6:4). In order for this new person to emerge, we must "lose the old person." The Bible states, "You were taught to put away your former way of life—your old self, corrupt and deluded by lusts, and to be renewed in the spirit of your minds, and to clothe yourselves with the new self, created according to the likeness of God in true righteousness and holiness" (Ephesians 4:22-24, NRSV). True spirituality begins with our lives being lost in the life of Christ.

Time for a Trade-In

How do we exchange the old "I" for the new? How do we make the statement in Galatians 2:20 (KJV), "I live; yet not I...." a practical reality for our own lives?

God cannot change us until we admit that we need God's help. We must acknowledge our need for change. The old "I" is in trouble. It must be transformed through the power of the Gospel of Jesus Christ.

"Very truly, I tell you, unless a grain of wheat falls into the earth and dies, it remains just a single grain; but if it dies, it bears much fruit. Those who love their life lose it, and those who hate their life in this world will keep it for eternal life" (John 12:24-25, NRSV). So it is in the life of the believer. Just as the seed must die to bear fruit, to find eternal life you must lose your life in Christ. If we are going to produce the fruit of the Spirit, we must die to ourselves—to the wants, desires, and concerns of the flesh. God has something better for us in Christ. The old "I," the human ego, must be lost if we are going to find the true spiritual "I" that demonstrates the love and power of God.

"If any one be in Christ [they] are a new creation; old things are passed away, behold everything has become new" (2 Corinthians 5:17, NRSV). To trade in the old for the new, we need to surrender. We must lose the old "I" to receive the new; give it up and let it go. The old "I" can be exchanged when we affirm and trust in what God has done for us in Christ. God offers us new life and a fresh beginning. "God was in Christ reconciling the world unto Himself" (2 Corinthians 5:19, NRSV). God has done everything for us so that we can live the life to which He has called us. The real freedom and power of the believer comes in giving up his or her life for the life of Christ.

New and Free

Being in Christ is liberating. When we lose the old "I"—the "I" that binds us to old habits and old ways—we then can be free to live the way God wants us to live. "So if the Son makes you free, you will be free indeed" (John 8:36, NRSV). Our freedom was won at a great price—the price of our Lord's death. God has purchased our freedom so that the work of God can be done in our lives. It is when we recognize this that our true sense of freedom comes forth as the morning's sunrise. True freedom can only be found in Jesus Christ.

New and Power-Filled

Being in Christ is also empowering. We are set free and then empowered to live for God. The Law was unable to empower us. In fact, it did quite the opposite; it bound us to customs and traditions that could not strengthen us to do God's holy will. "It is no longer I who live, but it is Christ who lives in me" (Galatians 2:20, NRSV). *"Christ lives in me"*—what a statement of empowerment! We have the very presence of the indwelling Christ in our lives to help us and strengthen us to be and do all that God has called us to be in Christ.

Living in Christ

You may ask, "What difference does all this make in the life of the Christian?" Furthermore, "What difference will it make in our human circumstances?"

The new "I" has been transformed, made whole, healed, infused with the power and love of God. The new "I" seeks to please God. This new "I," which is in Jesus Christ, reaches out to others in love and in prayer; it is filled with hope and courage. It lifts up the downtrodden; it feeds the hungry; it clothes the naked; it speaks the truth in love. The new "I" has been empowered by the Holy Spirit to live a new way of life.

The new "I" in Jesus Christ looks forward to the future in faith, constantly being renewed and energized by the power and presence of the Holy Spirit. We cannot live the Christian life without being in Christ. God gives us new hope, new love, new joy, new strength, and new life, so that we can live for Christ. It is this transformation which will make all the difference in the life of the believer, in the believer's interactions with others, and in the world around us.

Because we now live in Christ, we have the potential to live our lives above the mundane and the commonplace. We have the ability to reach new spiritual plateaus. We have a new awareness and sensitivity to the ever-abiding presence of God operating in our lives and reaching through us to touch the lives of others.

BIBLE STUDY APPLICATION

Being Hidden in Christ

In order to enjoy the fullness of Christian living, we must unite ourselves totally with Christ; we must allow ourselves to be lost in Him. Our identification with Christ comes from the surrender of our lives to Him and not from our good works. We must die to ourselves and allow the Holy Spirit to fill our lives.

1. Read Isaiah 53:4-11. Use these verses to answer the following questions.
   a) What's wrong with the old "I"?
   b) Why did Christ die for us?

2. Read Romans 1:18-32. Use these verses to answer the following questions.
   a) What's wrong with the old "I"?
   b) Why are we "without excuse"?

3. Read Romans 3:10-20. Use these verses to answer the following questions.
   a) What's wrong with the old "I"?
   b) Are some of us better than others in the sight of God?

4. Read Romans 3:21-26. Use these verses to answer the following questions.
   a) What's wrong with the old "I"?
   b) Are we justified by the Law or by grace?

5. Read Romans 6:3-11. Use these verses to answer the following questions.
   a) What has happened to your old life?
   b) From what have we been made free?
   c) To what have we been made alive?

6. Read 2 Corinthians 5:14-21. Use these verses to answer the following questions.
   a) What has happened to your old life?
   b) How do we receive new life?

7. Read Galatians 2:19-20. Use these verses to answer the following questions.
   a) What has happened to your old life?
   b) How do we live the new life?

8. Read Ephesians 2:4-10. Use these verses to answer the following questions.
   a) How have we been made "alive together with Christ"?
   b) Why can't a Christian ever truthfully say that he or she is a self-made man or woman?
   c) Once we have accepted God's gift of salvation, how should this truth affect the way we live?

9. Read Colossians 3:1-4. Use these verses to answer the following questions.
   a) How does our new life affect our goals?
   b) How does our new life affect our thoughts?
   c) How does our new life affect our expected rewards?

10. Read the words of Jesus in Mark 8:35. Explain what this verse means in light of Paul's teachings about our life in Christ.

PERSONAL APPLICATION

1. Whose life is it? Has there been a time in your life when you have voluntarily handed your life over to God?

2. If yes, describe the experience. If no, would you prayerfully consider surrendering your life now?

3. What things have changed in your life since you became a Christian?

4. If you had a problem being prideful, how would the truth of Galatians 2:20 help you overcome it?

5. How can you respond to those who think that "it doesn't take all that?"

CHURCH MINISTRY APPLICATION

1. The concept of being in Christ is both liberating (John 8:31-32) and empowering (1:12-13).
   a) How can the Church help the congregation to understand and experience freedom in Christ?
   b) How can the Church help the congregation to understand and experience the power of the indwelling Holy Spirit in their lives?

2. The concept of abiding in Christ is central to the life of the Christian. Read John 15:4-8. How can the Church help to equip the believer to abide in Christ?

3. As we move from the self-life to the life of Christ or the Christian life, we become fruitful. How can the Church provide the enrichment that increases fruit-bearing?

Holy Spirit, Come!
(1940)

Holy Spirit, come, possess me;
My whole being elevate.
As I search the Holy Scriptures,
Or in rapture meditate.

Make my thinking wise and reverent;
Let me see with vision clear;
Touch my lips, that I proclaim
Truth inspired, void of fear.

Fit me for my holy calling;
Make me harmless as a dove;
In the likeness of the Master,
Let me serve, with heart of love.

Give me grace, when wronged, to suffer,
Treading in the Savior's steps;
Fill my soul with God-like pity,
In its fulness and its depths.

Crown with blessing all my labors,
Every day and every where,
As I serve in home or temple,
Giving counsel, or in prayer.[8]

—Walter Henderson Brooks

CHAPTER FOUR

POWER FROM ON HIGH

"Whites Only." "Coloreds to the Back of the Bus." These were signs of the times in the 1940s and '50s. As a race, we saw our fathers and brothers hunted, beaten, and lynched. We saw our sisters degraded and raped. And we watched as our mothers served white households to make ends meet. For too long, we watched, powerless to interfere or to change things.

Until the '60s, when new signs arose—signs that proclaimed "Black Power" and "Power to the People." As a race, we realized that we did have the power and the courage to act. We watched the Black Panther Movement fight racism with physical weapons. We saw the Nonviolent Movement fight discrimination with spiritual weapons. And change was made.

On April 16, 1963, Martin Luther King, Jr. wrote the following words from a Birmingham, Alabama jail cell:

"There was a time when the Church was very powerful. It was during that period when the early Christians rejoiced when they were deemed worthy to suffer for what they believed. In those days the Church was not merely a thermometer that recorded the ideas and principles of popular opinion; it was a thermostat that transformed the mores of society. Wherever the early Christians entered a town the power structure got disturbed and immediately sought to convict them for being 'disturbers of the peace' and 'outside agitators.' But they went on with the conviction that they were a 'colony of heaven' and had to obey God rather than man. They were small in number but big in commitment. They were too God-intoxicated to be 'astronomically intimidated.' They brought an end to such ancient evils as infanticide and gladiatorial contest.

"Things are different now. The contemporary Church is so often a weak, ineffectual voice with an uncertain sound. It is so often the arch-supporter of the status quo. Far from being disturbed by the presence of the Church, the power structure of the average community is consoled by the Church's silent and often vocal sanction of things as they are.

"But the judgment of God is upon the Church as never before. If the Church of today does not recapture the sacrificial spirit of the early Church, it will lose its authentic ring, forfeit the loyalty of millions, and be dismissed as an irrelevant social club with no meaning for the twentieth century. I am meeting young people every day whose disappointment with the Church has risen to outright disgust.

"Maybe I have been too optimistic. Is organized religion too inextricably bound to the status quo to save our nation and the world? Maybe

I should turn my faith to the inner spiritual Church, the church within the Church, as the true ecclesia and the hope of the world."[9]

Today, as believers in Christ, we are more than just the members of a religious or a social organization. We have been called to change the world. We must realize that we have the power to make a difference. Our power is not ordinary human power, it is the power of God. We must put this power into action.

As we walk and witness in the power of the Holy Spirit, the "spiritual Church" can be the ray of hope for the world. How we express our faith to the people of our community will, in large part, determine how far we will go and what we will become in the future. God is still able to transform individuals and communities. By the power of the Holy Spirit, we can become God's instruments of change in this world.

A New Pentecost
Acts 1:3-9; 2:1-4

After his suffering, he showed himself to these men and gave many convincing proofs that he was alive. He appeared to them over a period of forty days and spoke about the kingdom of God. On one occasion, while he was eating with them, he gave them this command: "Do not leave Jerusalem, but wait for the gift my Father promised, which you have heard me speak about. For John baptized with water, but in a few days you will be baptized with the Holy Spirit."

So when they met together, they asked him, "Lord, are you at this time going to restore the kingdom to Israel?" He said to them: "It is not for you to know the times or dates the Father has set by his own authority. But you will receive power when the Holy Spirit comes on you; and you will be my witnesses in Jerusalem, and in all Judea and Samaria, and to the ends of the earth."

After he said this, he was taken up before their very eyes, and a cloud hid him from their sight.

When the day of Pentecost came, they were all together in one place. Suddenly a sound like the blowing of a violent wind came from heaven and filled the whole house where they were sitting. They saw what seemed to be tongues of fire that separated and came to rest on each of them. All of them were filled with the Holy Spirit and began to speak in other tongues as the Spirit enabled them.

Do you want power? I mean real power. The world defines power as the ability to control other people's lives. However, when Christians speak of power we are talking about another matter all together. The word for power in the New Testament is *dunamis*. It has the same root as the word "dynamite." However, this is not an ordinary power. It is the same power that raised Christ from the dead (1 Peter 3:18). It is the power of God in the person of the Holy Spirit.

Waiting for the Promise

We all like to know what's going to happen next. In Acts chapter 1, the resurrected Lord instructed the disciples to wait in Jerusalem for the promise of the Father. Then He went back to heaven. The disciples did not know what to expect. They didn't really know what the Holy Spirit was or what they were going to do. They had no idea. They just obeyed the words of Jesus, and they went back and waited.

There were approximately 120 men and women together in the upper room. They spent much time in prayer (Acts 1:14). But in addition they must have spent some time talking about Jesus. They were talking about the miracles He performed, the 5,000 people He fed, and the multitudes He healed. They were remembering how He taught them to love one another. They were discussing how He promised to go to prepare a place for them, and how they believed that He would come back again soon. They were waiting for God to act.

We don't like to wait. We're impatient. We like to make our own agenda. We even put it on graphs and charts and show it to everyone else. And we think we have the power to execute it. We think we have the power of implementation. When all along, as the people of God, we should be waiting for God's agenda.

Sometimes, all we can do is wait for God to act. That's all, just wait. Maybe you've been praying for somebody—a child, friend, or a husband or wife—and nothing seems to be happening. But the Lord didn't say every time you bend your knee and bow your head that He was going to act at that very moment. He just says wait. Just wait. Wait on the Lord.

Many times, the best thing to do is to do nothing. For example, when somebody says or does something that you don't like, let God have it. Let God take care of it. You don't have to defend yourself if you belong to Jesus. Just keep on doing what God has told you to do. God will be your defense. God will take care of you.

When God acts, you know something's going to happen. When we act, we mess it up. We fumble. We stumble. But when God acts, it's straight up. It's solid.

The Importance of Unity

On the Day of Pentecost, the believers were all together in one place. Think about that. They didn't have little groups here and there. There wasn't one group with their own agenda over in one corner and another group with their agenda in a different corner. They were "all with one accord in one place" (Acts 2:1, KJV). In other words, they were together both literally and figuratively.

As God's people, we must discover the importance of having both natural and spiritual unity. If the Holy Spirit is going to renew our hearts and minds, shake us up and put us back together again, and send us out to be a mighty force in our world; we must be all together in one place.

The Work of the Spirit

As the believers waited together, the sound of a violent wind from heaven suddenly filled the entire house. The wind is used to symbolize the Holy Spirit in both the Old and the New Testaments. The description of the wind in this passage speaks of power. The Bible says the sound was as a "violent wind" (2:2)—that's tornado talk; it's hurricane language. The term "violent wind" also describes the movement of God's Spirit. The wind of the Holy Spirit can knock down our idols—the things that we worship, the things we put before God. Whether it is a home, a car, a job, clothes, a bank account, or another person—whatever it is, we must let it go. We must put God first. We need the Holy Spirit to move in our churches and our communities to tear down those things that are destroying us and build up the things that can help us.

After the sound of the wind, what looked like tongues of fire appeared among the believers (2:3). The fire split apart and a tongue of fire rested upon each of them. These tongues of fire point to the work of the Holy Spirit in the life of the believer. The Holy Spirit makes each believer new from the inside out. He removes bad attitudes, selfishness, greed, and false pride. He takes away unforgiveness, hatred, and racism. He burns it out. The Holy Spirit purifies our soul so that we can become the people that we ought to be.

Filled and Speaking the Language

As the believers were filled with the Spirit, they began to speak in other tongues and other languages as the Spirit gave them the ability (2:4). The word "filled" simply means controlled. It means that they came under the complete control and absolute authority of the Holy Spirit.

People from all over the world were gathered in Jerusalem to celebrate the Passover. As the believers began to speak in the power of the Holy Spirit, the Bible says that those who heard them said, "Why, they are speaking in our language!" (Acts 2:7-11, paraphrased) Some of the believers spoke in Asian languages, and some spoke in Latin languages, and some spoke in African languages and dialects. The Holy Spirit enabled these uneducated believers to speak in languages that other people could understand.

We also must learn to speak the language of the people. We need to relate to people where they are. Sometimes, we talk below people and we insult their intelligence. Too often, we talk above people to show how smart we are. However, we must learn to talk with people in the power of the Spirit. The Holy Spirit will give us the ability to speak of heavenly things in the language that others can hear and understand.

The presence and the power of the Holy Spirit gave Peter new boldness. Instead of denying the Lord, he was able to stand up and preach the Gospel with power (2:14-42). Something had happened to him on the inside. The presence of the Holy Spirit changed Peter, and he took on a new character.

The Spirit can do the same thing for you. He gives us a new courage and the power to witness. He enables us to speak with boldness to those around us. When was the last time you talked to somebody about Jesus? When was the last time you spoke to your co-worker or your neighbor about Jesus Christ? When was the last time you said something to your family members about the love of God and what God can do in their lives?

When the Spirit Comes

The Day of Pentecost represented the infusion of new life into God's people. We must seek just such an infusion today. We need a new Pentecost. We need to see the power and the presence of the Holy Spirit released in our communities, freeing alcoholics, drug addicts, and prostitutes. We need the power of the Holy Spirit in the lives of young children who are battered and abused, who are damaged from life in dysfunctional or broken homes. We need the presence of the Holy Spirit to come into the lives of those who have nowhere to go and no place to turn, no hope for tomorrow and no promise in their heart for a better day.

The Holy Spirit brings real life-changing, life-giving power. When the Holy Spirit comes, people are converted. They are turned around. New attitudes develop. Old habits disappear. The Holy Spirit gives believers in Christ a new vision, a new direction, and a new purpose. He separates us to do God's will. He empowers us to go out and do God's work in a dying and sinful world.

When we are empowered by the Spirit it is evident.

What are the signs? First, our priorities are in order. We put first things first. We avoid the distractions and seductions of the world. Jesus said, "Seek ye first the kingdom of God, and his righteousness; and all these things shall be added unto you" (Matthew 6:33, KJV). There is a sense of balance in our lives—a "centering down" of our spirits. We become God's witnesses, first at home, then in our community, and finally in the world.

Second, our values are clearer. We know what to hold on to and what to cast aside. We have a new perspective on living. We develop a new value system predicated on our relationship with God.

Third, our direction is set. We know where we are going because God is leading. Sometimes life can seem like a maze; but when we put our trust in the Lord, we go in the right direction. "He leads me beside still waters" (Psalm 23:2b, NRSV). The Holy Spirit leads us to a new calmness of mind and spirit. He leads us to a new understanding of ourselves and our relationships with others. The Holy Spirit not only leads us, He enables us to follow. He gives us His power so that we can say, "Where He leads me, I will follow."

The Church of Jesus Christ must look to the power and presence of the Holy Spirit if we are going to transform the society in which we live. The promise of the Father has been fulfilled. As we allow the wind and the fire of the Holy Spirit to stir our hearts and minds, we will stand up in the power of the Spirit and tell the people that they can be delivered, healed, lifted up, and set free. We will proclaim that they can find forgiveness for their sins in Jesus Christ. We will tell them that Jesus Christ is the hope of the world, and that He's coming again to establish a new order, a new kingdom, a new way of life, a new reality. And we will see the power of God changing hearts and lives.

Do you want this power? Holy Ghost power. Healing power. Forgiving power. Saving power. Sanctifying power. This is what we need today. We need a new Pentecostal experience. Let us ask the Holy Spirit to fill our cup. We must let the Holy Spirit have His way. Let us allow the Holy Spirit to do His work in our lives so that we will receive power from on high.

BIBLE STUDY APPLICATION

Heirs of the Kingdom

Jesus' method of establishing the kingdom of God was not based on changing the existing political, economic, or social structure. It was based on changing the human heart by the power of the Holy Spirit.

1. Use the verses in parentheses to answer the following questions concerning the nature of God's kingdom.
   a) Describe the characteristics of the kingdom of God. (Romans 14:17; 1 Corinthians 4:20)
   b) Where is the kingdom of God? (Luke 17:20-21)
   c) How do we enter the kingdom of God? (John 3:3, 5-6)

2. Match the following verses to their description of the coming of the Holy Spirit.
   a. Joel 2:28-29; Acts 2:17, 18
   b. Matthew 3:11
   c. Luke 14:49
   ____Clothed with power from on high
   ____Baptized with the Holy Spirit and with fire

_____Poured out on all flesh

3. Use the following verses to describe how the Holy Spirit was sent to believers.

    a) In whose name or under whose authority was the Holy Spirit sent to believers? (John 14:26)

    b) From where did the Holy Spirit come? (John 15:26)

4. Read Romans 8:14-17. Use these verses to describe how we know that we are the children of God.

    a) Verse 9

    b) Verse 14

    c) Verse 16

Possessors of Power

The disciples waited in Jerusalem for the promised Holy Spirit. Today, the power of Holy Spirit is available to every believer.

5. The Holy Spirit is called the "promise of the Father." Use the verses in parentheses to answer the following questions about receiving God's promise.

    a) To whom is the Holy Spirit promised? (Acts 2:39)

    b) How do we receive the Holy Spirit? (Galatians 3:14)

    c) When do we receive the Holy Spirit? (Ephesians 1:13)

    d) How can we identify the Holy Spirit? (John 16:14; 1 John 4:1-2)

    e) How long will the Holy Spirit abide with us? (John 14:16)

6. Describe the work of the Holy Spirit in the life of the believer.
    a) 1 Corinthians 6:11
    b) 1 John 3:24; 4:13
    c) Romans 8:14
    d) Ephesians 3:16; Colossians 1:11
    e) Matthew 10:20; 1 Corinthians 2:4
    f) Romans 8:26-27
    g) Romans 15:13

7. Use the following verses to identify other ways that the power of the Holy Spirit is exhibited.
    a) Genesis 1:2
    b) Luke 1:35
    c) Romans 15:19
    d) 1 Peter 3:18

Witnesses for Jesus

A witness is one who tells what he or she has heard, seen, or experienced. It is the power of the Holy Spirit which makes our witness for Jesus Christ effective in the lives of others.

8. As believers in Christ, we are called to share the Gospel. What is the Gospel? (1 Corinthians 15:3-4)

9. Use the following verses to describe how the Holy Spirit empowers our witness.
    a) Acts 2:37; 16:14
    b) John 16:7-8
    c) John 14:16; 4:26
    d) Romans 1:16; 1 Thessalonians 1:5

10. We can learn much from the account of Jesus witnessing to the woman of Samaria. Read John 4:4-30, 39-42. Identify which verse(s) show that:

    a) Jesus "spoke her language" and opened the conversation on a subject that was familiar to her.

    b) He turned the conversation from natural (physical) things to spiritual things.

    c) He brought her to recognize the fact of her sin.

    d) He revealed Himself as Christ.

    e) His witness produced results. She became a believer and brought others to Christ.

PERSONAL APPLICATION

1. Do you have the power of the Holy Spirit in your life? If not, do you want this power?

2. Can you describe the difference between natural (physical) power and spiritual power? Can you distinguish between the kingdoms of the world and the kingdom of God?

3. Did you realize that a believer is never really alone? We have the Holy Spirit as our constant companion. How does this truth affect your daily life?

4. When you think about witnessing for Jesus Christ, how do you react? (Either check the appropriate sentence(s), or write one of your own.)

    _____I find it difficult to talk about such a personal matter.

    _____I only speak if someone asks me.

_____I find it easy to talk about Christ with people whom I know.

_____I find it easier to talk with strangers than with family or close friends.

_____I often find myself talking to people about Christ, and I enjoy it very much.

5. By depending on the power of the Holy Spirit and leaving the results to Him, witnessing simply becomes a matter of love and obedience. How will this perspective change your attitude toward witnessing?

CHURCH MINISTRY APPLICATION

1. How can the Church support or facilitate the work of the Holy Spirit in the lives of its members?

2. How can different church groups and the individual members be encouraged to develop unity?

3. Read 2 Corinthians 12:9 and 2 Timothy 1:7-8. Identify the weaker areas of church ministry. Pray that the power of the Holy Spirit and the plan of God be revealed in these areas.

The Pattern of Prayer

He is Creator, Giver of Life, Sustainer of Life, Redeemer, Judge, Righteous Will, Friend, Companion. A recognition of God brings with it a feeling and a thought of one's attitude toward One who is regarded as Creator and Redeemer. This mood is most naturally expressed in some form of thanksgiving and praise. It is important to say that such a feeling is most natural—it is not to suggest merely that God requires it. The mood of thanksgiving inspires an awareness of individual shortcomings and failures expressing themselves in contrition, confession and a deep desire for forgiveness. Forgiveness nets a sense of being cleansed, purified, which cleansing and purification must be spelled out in the fabric of one's living by the changes in behavior which undergird the sense of cleansing. There follows quite normally the sharing of one's personal desires, hopes and needs with One who understands. These longings are usually cast in the form of personal petitions of one kind or another. What enters here comes under the scrutiny of God, and often many changes, even in their form, take place. From this step, it is simple to move to the sharing of one's desires and hopes for others, and one's sense of need which the whole human family shares—the need for peace, for health, for justice and for decency. Once these are deeply shared with God, it becomes clear at what points one must share with God in the whole task of redeeming human life. Of course, this pattern of prayer that has evolved does not take into account those spontaneous outpourings of the heart and mind to God. Prayer at its best is revealed when a man enjoys God and prays out of sheer love of Him.[10]

—*Howard Thurman*

CHAPTER FIVE

THE PURPOSE OF PRAYER

"Get ready. Get set. Go!" It's as if an unseen announcer begins the countdown. Like a shot, the alarm goes off. The human race is living up to its name. Run, run, run— we are busier than ever. Some of us stumble out of the starting blocks; we hit the snooze button or turn over, trying to get a few more minutes of sleep. Others run slowly until they've had their morning cup of coffee. But run we do.

What's your course like? Does it start with children to dress or commuter traffic? Are you running under pressure? Do you hear the refrain "don't be late" in mental stereo sound? It's almost like playing beat the clock with a never-ending list of things to do. How can we keep pace?

Often life demands so much from us that we are no longer able to serve others effectively. We do, we go, we expend our time, talent, and our physical and spiritual resources trying to meet the demands of this fast-paced world in which we live. Unfortunately, too many of us are running on empty. We all need solitary moments where we can be refreshed. If we are to continue to give, we must be refilled.

Where can we find release and relief? An old hymn

71

with an ever-meaningful message states, "I come to the garden alone." It is in this lonely, quiet place—this place of prayer—that we come to understand what it means to be in the presence of the Almighty God who loves us and sustains us. Prayer is the place where we can meet God face to face. It is the place where God Himself ministers to our needs and enables us to reach out to others in the name of Jesus Christ. In the garden of prayer, God infuses our lives with the inner healing and strength that only He can give. Because He meets us there, we receive His power for living.

We must know how to find that place of quiet and rest, near to the heart of God. When we meet with God in prayer, He will meet our every need and strengthen us to do His will. Don't run on empty. God provides free refills for us. Meet God in the garden of prayer.

The Blessedness of a Lonely Place

Mark 1:32-39

That evening after sunset the people brought to Jesus all the sick and demon-possessed. The whole town gathered at the door, and Jesus healed many who had various diseases. He also drove out many demons, but he would not let the demons speak because they knew who he was.

Very early in the morning, while it was still dark, Jesus got up, left the house and went off to a solitary place, where he prayed. Simon and his companions went to look for him, and when they found him, they exclaimed:

"Everyone is looking for you!"

Jesus replied, "Let us go somewhere else—to the near-by villages— so I can preach there also. That is why I have come." So he traveled throughout Galilee, preaching in their synagogues and driving out demons.

People come to church for various reasons. Some to be quiet, some to escape, some to be refreshed, some to reexamine life, some to sing, some to usher, others to observe. Some may have come out of curiosity. Some have discovered how fragile they were in the past week. Others may have discovered some human deficiency within themselves. Many have faced adverse circumstances in life. Some may have lost a loved one or had someone they know suffer illness. Each day, we face a variety of circumstances that strain our souls. Where do we go for relief, for comfort, or for solace?

Many have tried different escape routes. Some look for more fun and thrills, while others bury themselves in overwork. Some engage in dangerous activities that lead to self-destruction, while others create a world of pure fantasy and get lost in silly illusions—pretending to be someone other than who they are.

People have a need to get away from it all. Some call it trying to find themselves. The word "burnout" has become very popular in recent years. Under the stresses and strains of life, people suffer from depersonalization and derealization; they lose the point of their own identity and importance. People need to regain a focus in life. There is, by necessity, something within our souls that demands rest. The big question is, how do we find rest in a restless world?

Life is not fair, and it is not meant to be. We are fragmented by responsibilities and adversities. When we look around us and see the needs and pains of life, we wonder if everything will eventually fall into place. It is like trying to put the pieces of a puzzle together—the more we try, the harder it becomes. To whom do we turn to find help? To whom do we turn to help us put the pieces of our lives back together again?

The Example of Our Lord

Even Jesus needed to get away from the crowd. Mark 1:32-39 gives us some very poignant glimpses into the inner personality of our Lord. The human side of our Lord needed to be strengthened and refreshed. Jesus had spent the greater part of a day meeting the needs of people. He had been working vigorously—exorcising demons and healing all manner of diseases. He was using a lot of spiritual energy preaching the Good News of the Gospel to people who were in need. After preaching and teaching, healing the sick, and casting out demons, Jesus needed to be renewed. He must have been exhausted. He had to find a place away from the crowd. Thus, in the early morning hours of this particular day, while it was still dark, He stole away from His disciples to pray.

Jesus knew that He had to have a secret place, a place between the world and Himself. "He that dwelleth in the secret place of the most High shall abide under the shadow of the Almighty. I will say of the Lord, He is my refuge and my fortress: my God; in him will I trust" (Psalm 91:1-2, KJV). Our Lord went to be strengthened and refreshed in the presence of God. Jesus needed to be empowered to do the work God had sent Him to do. He chose a deserted, solitary spot to meet with God in prayer.

The fact that Jesus prayed, as well as the content of Jesus' prayer, shows clearly that we ourselves need to pray. How often on our spiritual journey do we desire such a place, a hiding place where we can regain both our physical and spiritual strength? People are still in need, and the only way we can meet their needs is to be prepared ourselves. Have you ever been tired and didn't know why? It is no wonder; there are forces working to oppose you, and you need all the strength you can get.

Sometimes we have to close the door on our busy world and just commune with God. We must let go of everything. When you pray, enter into your "closet" in secret (Matthew 6:6, KJV). Solitude is sometimes necessary in order for us to replenish our inner resources. Our time alone with God enables us to face the challenges created by life's everyday circumstances. Like Jesus, we need to find that secret place under the shadow of the Almighty. There we will find solitude and rest, and we will receive strength to do God's will.

What Is Prayer?

Prayer is the essence of the soul's communion with the Holy God; it is the highest activity of the mind and spirit. In prayer, we open our soul to the unseen author of its environment, God. The psalmist cries out, "My soul thirsts . . . for the living God" (Psalm 42:2). It is in and through prayer that we discover a new spiritual dimension—a new level of spiritual awareness which brings the soul near to the heart of the living God.

> There is a place of quiet rest, near to the heart
> of God
> A place where sin cannot molest, near to the
> heart of God.
> There is a place of comfort sweet, near to the
> heart of God;
> A place where we our Savior meet, near to the

Rev 7th Chp.
Space for ½ hr.

heart of God.

There is a place of full release, near to the heart of God;

A place where all is joy and peace, near to the heart of God.

O Jesus, blest redeemer, sent from the heart of God;

Hold us who wait before thee, near to the heart of God.[11]

In prayer, the soul rises to meet its God in the heavens. The prayer of petition beseeches God's blessings upon us. The prayer of intercession entreats God to bless others. The prayer of thanksgiving or praise displays our adoration of who God is and what God has done for us in Jesus Christ. The highest form of prayer is the prayer of contemplation or meditation. This prayer is a pondering of the transcendent—the infinite and imminent presence of the living God. As we meditate on the divine nature and love of God, our soul is lifted to a new awareness of and delight in God's presence with us.

We know that the Word is important for Christian living; reading the Bible and allowing it to speak to our hearts will bring the direction we need in life. Fellowship is important; God gives us a spiritual family who may bring support to us in time of difficulty. God gives us people who can understand our need to allow God to work in our lives. God gives us still others upon whom we can call and ask to pray with us and for us.

However, the importance of private prayer can never be overestimated. People need time with God in prayer. We need God's presence and power to refresh our weary spirits and strengthen our burdened hearts. It is often in these quiet moments of prayer that we most strongly sense the power and presence of God.

What Happens in Prayer?

In prayer, we bring before an Almighty God our most basic selves and all that we have. We bring our needs, our hurts and pains, and the storms that rage in our souls. The words to that old hymn of the church remind us where we need to go:

> From every stormy wind that blows,
> From ev'ry swelling tide of woes.
> There is a calm, a sure retreat;
> 'Tis found beneath the mercy seat.
>
> There, there on eagle wings we soar,
> And sin and sense molest no more;
> And heaven comes down, our souls to greet,
> And glory crowns the mercy seat.[12]

What happens when we find that quiet moment with God? We reassess our gains and losses. The moments we spend in the presence of God give us the opportunity to allow God's Spirit to search our hearts and minds. In His presence, we discover our limits and our cutting edges. Life can take so much from us, in so many ways. We need to get away and be alone with the Lord so that we can see ourselves as He sees us.

Our quiet time gives us the opportunity to reassess our resources. We can ask, "What do we have left?" In God's presence, we discover the infinite resources we have in God. We have God's Word. We have the consolation and the promise of the Scriptures: "The Lord is my Shepherd; the Lord is my light and my salvation; God is my refuge and strength." The Word of God assures us of an inexhaustible supply of God's grace and love. In prayer, God reminds us of the Word and provides the wisdom and direction that we need.

In our quiet moments with God, we discover the spiritual strength that comes when we place our confidence and trust in Him. If we "wait" before God, He will meet our every need. Waiting in the presence of God places us in the position to receive God's provision and His strength. "But those who wait upon the Lord shall renew their strength, they shall mount up with wings like eagles, they shall run and not be weary, they shall walk and not faint" (Isaiah 40:31, NRSV).

We must find a place of solitude to communicate with God and to allow Him to communicate with us. God can meet our needs and refresh our spirits. God can fill us and empower us. A spiritually weak Christian cannot meet the needs of a sin-sick world. Like Jesus, we must become spiritually equipped to do God's will. In prayer, there is an inexhaustible and renewable resource available to us. Make time alone with God a regular part of your spiritual journey.

BIBLE STUDY APPLICATION

Private Prayer Is Essential

Public prayer is necessary in the life of the church. Praying together as a family is necessary for the strength of the home. But private prayer is essential to the spiritual life of the individual.

1. In Matthew 6:5, what does Jesus say about those who pray to be seen by others?

2. In Matthew 6:6, what does Jesus say about those who pray to the Father in secret?

3. In Matthew 6:7-8, what does Jesus say about those who use vain repetitions in prayer (repeating the same prayer or saying the same phrases and words over and over again)?

The Lord's Prayer

Although commonly referred to as "The Lord's Prayer," Jesus' prayer in Matthew 6:9-13 is really a model for prayer that He gave to the disciples. Jesus was not telling the disciples to pray this prayer word for word. He was giving a pattern or set of principles for prayer that we can follow today.

4. Read Matthew 6:9-13. Match the following phrases with the principles that they illustrate.

_____Our Father which art in heaven

_____Hallowed be thy name

_____Thy kingdom come, thy will be done on earth as it is in heaven

_____Give us this day our daily bread

_____And forgive us for our debts

_____As we forgive our debtors

_____And lead us not into temptation, but deliver us from evil

_____For thine is the kingdom, and the power, and the glory, forever. Amen.

a. Put God's concerns first.
b. Come into His presence with praise and worship.
c. Confess your sins and ask for forgiveness.

d. Recognize that we have access to God because of our special relationship with Him.

e. Ask Him to meet our needs for today.

f. Leave His presence with praise and worship.

g. Ask God for help and wisdom to avoid or overcome life's trials and tests.

h. Remember to release any grudges we may hold against others.

The Principles and Privileges of Prayer

Some may regard prayer as a burdensome responsibility, when in fact it is a priceless privilege. As we follow the principles of the Word of God and the leading of the Holy Spirit, we will experience the benefits of answered prayer.

5. What does Matthew 7:11 say about the privilege of knowing God as our Father?

6. What does Psalm 100:4 say about the principle of praise?

7. What does Matthew 6:33 say about the principle of putting God first?

8. What does Matthew 18:21-35 say about the principle of forgiveness?

9. Read Philippians 4:6-7. Use these verses to answer the following questions.
     a) What are we to worry about?
     b) What are we to pray about?
     c) What is prayer?

· d) What is supplication?

e) Why should we give thanks when we pray? (See also Hebrews 11:6.)

f) If we refuse to worry and instead we pray about everything, what will we receive as a result?

10. Why can we be confident in God's supply? (Philippians 4:19)

PERSONAL APPLICATION

1. Why should you pray?

2. When is the best time for you to pray?

3. Do you have a place where you can go to be alone with the Lord in prayer?

4. Search your heart. Is there anyone you need to forgive?

5. Read 1 John 1:9. Have you taken everything to God in prayer?

CHURCH MINISTRY APPLICATION

1. The body of Christ is only as strong as its members. How can the Church help the congregation to make personal prayer a priority?

2. As we begin to pray in agreement with God's will, our prayers will expand beyond the level of our own personal needs.

a) What are some of the other things for which we

are encouraged to pray in the Word of God?
(Psalm 122:6; Luke 6:28; 10:2; 22:40;
Philippians 1:9; Colossians 4:3; 1 Timothy 2:1-
2; James 5:14-16)
b) How can the Church be encouraged to consider
God's agenda in prayer?

3. Even though we know that God knows best, sometimes
we prefer our plan and our schedule. How can the
Church's members be encouraged to trust God's plan
and His timing as they wait to receive answers to
prayer?

I Will Sing a New Song

The old song of my spirit has wearied itself out. It has long ago been learned by heart so that now it repeats itself over and over, bringing no added joy to my days or lift to my spirit. It is a good song, measured to a rhythm to which I am bound by ties of habit and timidity of mind. The words belong to old experiences which once sprang fresh as water from a mountain crevice fed by melting snows. But my life has passed beyond to other levels where the old song is meaningless. I demand of the old song that it meet the need of present urgencies. Also, I know that the work of the old song, perfect in its place, is not for the new demand!

I will sing a new song. As difficult as it is, I must learn the new song that is capable of meeting the new need. I must fashion new words born of all the new growth of my life, my mind and my spirit. I must prepare for new melodies that have been mine before, that all that is within me may lift my voice unto God. How I love the old familiarity of the wearied melody—how I shrink from the harsh discords of the new untried harmonies.

Teach me, my Father, that I might learn with the abandonment and enthusiasm of Jesus, the fresh new accent, the untried melody, to meet the need of the untried morrow. Thus, I may rejoice with each new day and delight my spirit in each fresh unfolding.

I will sing, this day, a new song unto Thee, O God.[13]

—Howard Thurman

THE REASON
WE SING

When television programs were in black and white, a young-looking announcer held the microphone before a teenage girl. "And how do you rate that record?" he asked. "I'll give it a nine," she gushed. "It's got a good beat, and I can dance to it!" Like many things, popular music changes with the times.

Today, we have MTV, VH-1, and BET music videos. Rap lyrics, record scratching, and vocal sounds accompany and enhance the beat. Often the video performance tells a story of its own. As we look past the beat, the melody, and the dramatic style of today's music, we must ask ourselves: "What is the world singing about?"

Music has always been inspired by relationships. But our culture seems to be saying: "What does love have to do with it?" Love songs have been replaced by songs about sexual relationships. What was formerly implied is now graphically illustrated. Negative human relationships are also showcased, and violent actions and attitudes that were rarely considered are now often communicated in song.

As believers in Christ, the Word of God encourages us to sing about the most important relationship of all—our relationship with God through Jesus Christ. The musical tastes of African American Christians encompass the entire spectrum of liturgical music styles: rap, gospel, spirituals, anthems, classical, and hymns. However, it is the *message* of the music that matters most.

In these changing times, the Lord gives us a new song to sing. Our music lifts us above the mundane circumstances of life toward a greater understanding of God's will and purpose for our lives.

Why do Christians sing? We sing because:

Singing provides another way that we can proclaim the love and grace of God.

Singing honors the name of the Lord.

Music encourages our hearts and spirits.

Singing brings us closer to the ever-abiding presence of the living God.

Sing a New Song

Psalm 96:1-9

Sing to the Lord a new song; sing to the Lord, all the earth. Sing to the Lord, praise his name; proclaim his salvation day after day. Declare his glory among the nations, his marvelous deeds among all peoples.

For great is the Lord and most worthy of praise; he is to be feared above all gods. For all the gods of the nations are idols, but the Lord made the heavens. Splendor and majesty are before him; strength and glory are in his sanctuary.

Ascribe to the Lord, O families of nations, ascribe to the Lord glory and strength. Ascribe to the Lord the glory due his name; bring an offering and come into his courts. Worship the Lord in the splendor of his holiness; tremble before him, all the earth.

Don't you wish you could sing? I mean really sing—sing like Paul Robeson, Jessye Norman, Kathleen Battle; sing like William Warfield, Marion Anderson, Leontyne Price; how about singing like Smokey Robinson, Marvin Gaye, Aretha Franklin; or like Roberta Martin, Shirley Caesar, or James Cleveland? It has been said that music is the universal language. We need music; it lifts the soul, inspires the heart, and clears the mind.

Music is an integral part of worship. In the African American worship experience, music helps prepare the heart and mind to receive the Word of God. It uplifts and inspires worshipers to consider the ways of God. The music of the church creates an atmosphere that makes it easier for prayers to be uttered and for the message of the sermon to be heard.

Just as music is used to enliven the worship service and set the stage for the sermon, it is also a means by which the burdened soul of a worshiper can find relief. When nothing else suffices, singing can often make the difference for the Christian.

Vocal music, or singing, can help us deal with some of the harsher realities of this life. Charles Albert Tindley penned the words to the anthem of faith entitled "Some Day."

> Beams of Heaven as I go,
> Thro' this wilderness below,
> Guide my feet in peaceful ways,
> Turn my midnights into days;
> When in the darkness I would grope,
> Faith always sees a star of hope,
> And soon from all life's grief and danger,
> I shall be free some day.[14]

Many of the spirituals sung today came out of the experience of slavery. It was through singing that the African American people were able to express their deepest longings. Songs that spoke of judgment, freedom, hope, and peace came out of the people's desire to have a closer walk with God. The spirituals also captured the feelings of a people enslaved—the hurts and pains of their brutal existence. The misery of their oppression caused them to sing out of their souls' experiences. They knew that even if they could not speak, they could sing.

Like the captured Israelites who asked themselves: "How could we sing the Lord's song in a foreign land?" (Psalm 137:4, NRSV) We may also wonder: "How could our ancestors sing the Lord's song in a strange land?" But sing they did. Our forefathers and mothers sang because the Lord gave them a song. In spite of their adversities, they understood that God was present with them. Even in the face of great and grave difficulty—in the midnight hours, the Lord gave them a new song that was capable of meeting the new need.

And today, as a people, we keep on singing. We sing when we are glad; we sing when we are sad. We sing when we are well; we sing when we are sick. We sing when we have money, and we sing when we have "no mo' money." We sing anthems. We sing gospel. We sing classics. We sing the blues. We sing popular music. We sing hymns. We sing until all is well.

The Good Old Songs

Remember the refrain: "Give me that ol' time religion. It was good enough for my mother, and it's good enough for me." We all, of course, grasp the significance of that song to some degree. That old time religion was good. However, there must come a time for reassessment and revitalization. This generation must have a "new time religion." We say this, not to totally negate the old or rob it of its meaning, but there must be the new as well.

Howard Thurman states in his book *Meditations of the Heart*, "I must sing a new song unto God."[15] The time will come when the old song has worn out; when its old and familiar refrain can no longer bring joy or lift the spirit. Life passes on to new levels where the old song is meaningless.

We must sing a new song. "What kind of music; what kind of new songs?" you may ask.

A New Song for a New Day

We must learn to sing a new song for a new day—for the new demands of an ever-changing life in an ever-changing world. Songs with new words which show the growth of our mind and our spirit. Songs with new melodies that have never been sung before, so that all that is within us can be expressed as we lift our voices unto God.

The songs and the music can be as unique as each believer and each circumstance or situation of life. As we offer our songs to Him, the Lord will give us new songs to help us endure life's hills and valleys, and its joys and sorrows (Psalm 40:3).

The Song of Joy

"O come, let us sing to the Lord; let us make a joyful noise to the rock of our salvation!" (Psalm 95:1, NRSV) The song of joy can be sung at any time. It can be sung when life goes well, and it can be sung when life is difficult. The Scriptures teach, "Weeping may linger for the night, but joy comes with the morning" (Psalm 30:5b,

NRSV).

Jesus said, "I have said these things to you so that my joy may be in you, and that your joy may be complete" (John 15:11, NRSV). Here is a joy that sustains us through the course of time. It is a joy that emerges even in times of sorrow. The song of joy comes from the abiding presence of the Almighty God. This joy comes from a vital relationship with the Lord, who brings to us the salvation we need.

The Song of Salvation

"I will lift up the cup of salvation and call on the name of the Lord" (Psalm 116:13, NRSV). The song of salvation is also a song of deliverance, because Jesus Christ came to bring forgiveness and healing to all who would believe in Him. Our full deliverance and healing are in the Lord. In fact, the Lord Jesus Christ is our salvation. "There is salvation in no one else, for there is no other name under heaven given among mortals by which we must be saved" (Acts 4:12, NRSV).

The song of salvation is offered as a symbol of appreciation to the Lord for all that He has done for us in Jesus. As we sing the new song of salvation, we will find everything we need in the Lord, who made us. And we will find that the Lord is worthy of praise.

The Song of Praise

"Let us come before his presence with thanksgiving; let us make a joyful noise to him with songs of praise!" (Psalm 95:2, NRSV) We sing the song of praise because the Lord is a great God. God rules and we are the people of God. The song of praise lifts our spirits in adoration of who God is and what He does.

We sing to let people know of God's goodness, greatness, and grace. The Lord gives us new songs of praise as we receive new mercies and blessings, as we overcome new obstacles and pressures, and as we grow in understanding and knowledge of Him. Our God is worthy of our praise because He gives us a new song.

The Song of the Redeemed

What is the name of the new song? It is the song of the redeemed.

> God gave me a song that the angels cannot sing.
> I've been washed in the blood of the crucified one;
> I've been redeemed.
> The Lord has been so good to me;
> he opened doors I could not see.
> Sometimes when I am feeling low,
> and there is no place for me to go.
> My father is rich in houses and land;
> he holds the power of the world in his hand.[16]

The new song can only be sung by those who know the Heavenly Composer. Do you know Him as Saviour and Lord? Do you know the song of the Lamb? It is the song of the Redeemer: "Worthy is the Lamb that was slain to receive power, and riches, and wisdom, and strength, and honour, and glory, and blessing. Blessing, and honour, and glory, and power, be unto him that sitteth upon the throne, and unto the Lamb for ever and ever" (Revelation 5:12, 13b, KJV).

Singing from the Heart

God put the language of music in the heart of humankind, particularly in the heart of the believer. Through our music, we can we lift our hearts and souls to God. The Word of God admonishes us to make melody in our hearts unto the Lord, and to sing psalms, hymns, and spiritual songs to God (Ephesians 5:19). As we offer up our heartfelt expression in song, we are drawn closer to the ever-abiding presence of the living God.

BIBLE STUDY APPLICATION

The Power of Praise

Like prayer, music is a powerful form of communication. In fact, musical lyrics can be viewed as speech intensified. As we worship and praise God in song, the music which results can change the atmosphere as well as the attitude of the heart.

1. Read 1 Samuel 16:14-16, 23. Use these verses to answer the following questions.
   a) Who was the musician?
   b) For whom was he playing?
   c) What type of music was played?
   d) What effect did the music have?

2. Read 2 Chronicles 20:20-22. Use these verses to answer the following questions.
   a) Who were the singers?
   b) To whom were they singing?
   c) What type of song was sung?
   d) What happened when they began to sing?

3. Read Acts 16:25-26. Use these verses to answer the following questions.
   a) Who were the singers?
   b) To whom were they singing?
   c) What type of song did they sing?
   d) What happened while they prayed and sang?

Singing a New Song

We have become new creatures in Christ (2 Corinthians 5:17). Through Christ, we have been given access to God by "a new and living way" (Hebrews 10:20). Each day we face new circumstances. As we obey God, we will experience His power, provision, and protection in new ways. It is no wonder that Scripture repeatedly exhorts us to sing a new song to the Lord.

4. Match the following Scripture references with the reasons they give for singing new songs to the Lord.
   a. Psalm 33:1-5
   b. Psalm 96:1-6
   c. Psalm 98:1-6
   d. Psalm 144:9-11
   e. Psalm 149:1-4
   f. Isaiah 42:10-13

   _____For God has done marvelous things.
   _____For the Word of the Lord is upright, and all His work is done in faithfulness.
   _____For great is the Lord and greatly to be praised.
   _____For God gives victory to kings and rescues His servant.
   _____For the Lord takes pleasure in His people, and He adorns the humble with victory.
   _____For the Lord shows Himself mighty against His foes.

93

Songs from the Heart

Music is an important form of human expression, but there is a difference between a good performance, excellent entertainment, and heartfelt praise. The music of the Church must be different. As believers in Christ, we are a chosen people, a royal priesthood, a holy nation, and a people who belong to God. Therefore, we must declare the praises of Him who has called us out of darkness into His wonderful light (1 Peter 2:9).

5. Read Ephesians 5:19 and Colossians 3:16. Use these verses to answer to the following questions.
   a) What are three ways that we are encouraged to speak or sing?
   b) Where should the songs and the melody come from?
   c) What type of attitude should we have when we sing to God?

6. Read Matthew 15:8 and John 4:23-24. Describe the importance of singing to God from our hearts.

On Earth as in Heaven

We often sing and pray, "Thy will be done on earth as it is in heaven." In the Book of Revelation, we get a glimpse of the fervent, new songs of praise that ring throughout heaven.

7. Read Revelation 5:8-9. Use these verses to answer the following questions.
   a) Who were the singers?
   b) To whom were they singing?
   c) What type of song did they sing?

8. Read Revelation 5:11-12. Use these verses to answer the following questions.
   - a) Who were the singers?
   - b) How were they singing?
   - c) To whom were they singing?
   - d) What type of song did they sing?

9. Read Revelation 5:13-14. Use these verses to answer the following questions.
   - a) Who were the singers?
   - b) To whom were they singing?
   - c) What type of song did they sing?

10. Read Revelation 14:1-3. Use these verses to answer the following questions.
    - a) Who were the singers?
    - b) What type of song did they sing?
    - c) Where did they sing their song?

11. Read Revelation 15:2-3. Use these verses to answer the following questions.
    - a) Who were the singers?
    - b) What instrument were they holding?
    - c) What type of song did they sing?
    - d) To whom were they singing?

PERSONAL APPLICATION

1. Check yourself. Do you really spend enough time singing praises to the Lord?

2. When you sing, do you really mean it?

3. How does God want His people to sing?

4. Why should we sing a new song?

5. God's grace is sufficient in every situation. What are some of the ways singing to the Lord can help the singer?

CHURCH MINISTRY APPLICATION

1. How can the Church help its members understand the importance of worshiping God in song?

2. Review the type of songs that are sung during worship services. Should new songs be added? Can more psalms be sung? How often are hymns or sacred songs included?

3. Review the words of the songs. Are the songs spiritual songs? Do they agree with God's Word and please (not grieve) the Holy Spirit?

The Humble Spirit

The humble spirit and the contrite heart
Thou givest to him who seekest with true devotion.

The humble spirit. I learn the meaning of the humble spirit from the earth. The earth takes into itself the rain, the heat of the sun, and it works with these gifts of life to bring the magic out of itself to be used for growth and sustenance of all living things. The earth is good because it takes what life gives, and within itself it uses its gifts to make life abound. It waits for fruition and gathers its fruit unto itself for more life and more growing. I shall learn of the earth the meaning of the humble spirit.

The contrite heart. I will yield all the hard places of my heart to the softening influence of the Spirit of God. Despite my pride, my pain and my vainglory, I will yield every stubborn bit of the cancerous growth in my heart to God until He makes my heart whole, one united outlet of His spirit. It will not be easy, not simple perphaps, but in the quietness I give up to Him all the lumps, the unresolved bit of me.

The humble spirit and contrite heart
Thou givest to him who seekest with true devotion.[17]

—*Howard Thurman*

CHAPTER SEVEN

LIVING IN THE SPIRIT

He awakens to the chill of the cold morning air. His senses are immediately alert to possible danger. He moves slowly; his limbs are stiff from his cramped sleeping position. He gathers his cardboard boxes and plastic bags and begins his daily journey. On the way, he checks some garbage containers looking for aluminum cans or maybe something to eat. He is homeless.

She awakens to the sound of distant sirens and voices shouting in a neighbor's apartment next door. She doesn't notice the noise as she lies in bed thinking. Her mind is on how much money she has left, and how she and her children will make it until the next check comes. She lives in the ghetto.

He awakens to the voice of his favorite radio announcer giving the traffic report. The bed is warm and comfortable. Reluctantly, he gets up and begins to get ready for work. He thinks of his wife and children, and he considers himself to be a good provider. He lives in a nice house in a middle class neighborhood.

She leisurely awakens to the warmth of sunshine and the sound of birds chirping outside her window. Soon there is a knock on the bedroom door. At her request, a servant enters with breakfast on a tray. As she eats slowly, her favorite music plays. She doesn't consider household or financial matters because she knows that they have been met. Instead, she thinks about meeting a friend for lunch at a country club. She lives in luxury.

Where do you live? When you wake up in the morning, what do you think about? As Christians, we have received a new dimension for living. Just as we have a natural life and we consider the things which are associated with our lifestyle, we who have been made alive spiritually consider the things of the Spirit.

The Christian life is a life lived by the Spirit of God. It is through the Holy Spirit's influence and power that we are able to be what God is calling us to be in these days. When Jesus speaks of the presence of the Holy Spirit in the life of the believer, He is speaking about more than a "tingling" sensation. It will take a new force, a new energy, and a new mind set to bring us out of the quicksand of violence, drugs, and death in our communities. This new force, new energy, and new mind set will spring forth from the work of the Holy Spirit.

As we continue this pilgrimage toward true spirituality, we must remember that we can live by the guidance and direction of the Holy Spirit. There is no need even to try to go it alone.

Living in the Spirit

Romans 8:1-8

Therefore, there is now no condemnation for those who are in Christ Jesus, because through Christ Jesus the law of the Spirit of life set me free from the law of sin and death. For what the law was powerless to do in that it was weakened by the sinful nature, God did by sending his own Son in the likeness of sinful man to be a sin offering. And so he condemned sin in sinful man, in order that the righteous requirements of the law might be fully met in us, who do not live according to the sinful nature but according to the Spirit.

Those who live according to the sinful nature have their minds set on what that nature desires; but those who live in accordance with the Spirit have their minds set on what the Spirit desires. The mind of sinful man is death, but the mind controlled by the Spirit is life and peace; the sinful mind is hostile to God. It does not submit to God's law, nor can it do so. Those controlled by the sinful nature cannot please God.

What does it mean to be a spiritual person living on the threshold of the 21st century? Are we ready to face the new challenges that lie before us? If we are going to face the challenges of tomorrow, we must be fully equipped to do what God wants us to do.

Without Christ, we are weak, fragile, sinful creatures who often stumble and fall. We fall because we do not have the right stuff within ourselves to stand. Without the power of the Holy Spirit, we struggle to be what God has called us to be. We struggle to live the lives we want to live. We struggle to meet the demands placed on us by others. However, we cannot succeed in doing so. Therefore,

101

God has provided help for us through Jesus Christ.

No Condemnation

In Paul's letter to the Romans, the apostle explains God's plan of salvation for the human race. In some detail, he outlines what God has done for us. He makes it very clear that God has made complete arrangements so that we can obtain salvation through Jesus Christ.

The Law, the righteous requirements of a Holy God, can never be met because the flesh is weak. The demands of the Law are too much for the individual believer. We cannot keep the Law because we are intrinsically unable to keep it. God knows our inability. He also knows what we need because He is God. "For God has done what the Law, weakened by the flesh, could not do: by sending his own Son in the likeness of sinful flesh, he condemned sin in the flesh" (Romans 8:3, NRSV). God has made it possible for us to live according to His will. Through Jesus Christ, we can be and do what God demands of us.

Just as we receive salvation through faith in the finished work of Jesus Christ, Jesus promised us an Advocate, a Counselor, a Heavenly Helper who would give us the power to live the Christian life. The Christian life can be lived only by the power and presence of the Holy Spirit. It is the presence of the Holy Spirit in our lives and in the life of the Church that provides the power to do God's will.

To live in the Spirit, we must make a full surrender of ourselves to God. To bear the fruit of the Spirit, we must make a complete commitment to Jesus Christ. As we bring our lives under the complete control of God's Holy Spirit, we will find a new power operating within.

Free from the Law

Living in the Spirit will set us free from the Law. "For the law of the Spirit of life in Christ Jesus has set you free from the law of sin and of death" (Romans 8:2, NRSV). The law of sin and death exposes us for what we really are—poor and helpless creatures. But, as believers in Christ, we live under a new law. We receive eternal life and abundant life. The power of the Holy Spirit or the Spirit of life supersedes the law of sin and death, thus offering us a new opportunity to live the life which God calls us to live.

A New Mind Set

Living in the Spirit will change you. "For those who live according to the flesh set their minds on the things of the flesh, but those who live according to the Spirit set their minds on the things of the Spirit" (Romans 8:5, NRSV). The Holy Spirit gives us a new mind set. As our minds are renewed, our attitudes will change. As our attitudes are changed, our actions will change. This change can come only when the energizing power of the Holy Spirit enters into the picture of our lives.

Living According to the Spirit

When we live in the Spirit, life is different. We seek to live for God in new and meaningful ways. We realize that the vital link is prayer. As we reach out to God in prayer, we glorify God and receive His power. We realize that where there is no prayer, there is no power. Where there is little prayer, there is little power. Where there is much prayer, there is much power.

Living in the Spirit means that we allow the Holy Spirit of God to produce the fruit of the Spirit in and through us. When we live in the Spirit, a love emerges which conquers fear, overcomes our anxieties, and gives our life spiritual momentum. This is the perfect love of God which casts out fear (1 John 4:18). We find a peace we never knew before, an inner poise and tranquillity of spirit and mind. Storms may come, but the ballast within is maintained—controlled by the Holy Spirit. The presence of the Holy Spirit assures us that God's power and grace are sufficient to meet our every need. We have a new confidence that God cares about us. Our confidence in God gives us a sense of well-being. The presence of the Holy Spirit also produces the fruit of self-control, which provides balance and victory in our daily living.

Living in the Spirit is not just a private matter. It affects the whole of our public service. As we live in the Spirit, we become sensitive to the people and circumstances around us. Our spirituality and social reality are interconnected; we cannot have one without the other because they work together. As our hearts are changed by the Holy Spirit, we will reach out to the homeless, the hungry, and the destitute to offer them new life and new hope in Jesus.

The witness of the Church depends on the power and presence of the Holy Spirit in the life of the individual believer and the Church. "For the one who is in you is greater than the one who is in the world" (1 John 4:4, NRSV). Jesus Christ promised that the Holy Spirit would empower us to take the Gospel into all the world. The power of God's Spirit enables us to touch other people and bring them into the fellowship of Jesus Christ.

As God's people, we must do the work of Him who called us out of darkness into His marvelous light. As we live in the Spirit, we will receive the guidance, direction, and power to succeed in accomplishing God's will for our lives, and we will become a powerful people who are able to help others live their lives for God.

BIBLE STUDY APPLICATION

A Better Way

The Law was perfect and holy, but humankind is imperfect and carnal. The Israelites struggled in vain to keep the commandments. Thank God, there is a better way! Through Jesus Christ, God has condemned sin and at the same time made it possible for us to escape condemnation.

1. Read Jeremiah 31:31-33 and Hebrews 8:6-10. Use these verses to answer the following questions.
   a) What is different about the new covenant?
   b) Where is the Law in the new covenant?

2. Read Ezekiel 36:26-27. Use these verses to answer the following questions.
   a) What will God give us?
   b) What will He take away?
   c) What else will God give us?
   d) What will His Spirit within us cause us to do?

3. Why do you think that Paul uses the term "the law of the Spirit of life"? (1 John 5:11-13; 2 Corinthians 2:6)

4. Why do you think that Paul uses the term "the law of sin and death"? (Romans 3:23 and 6:23)

5. Why has God made it possible for us to escape condemnation? (John 3:16; 1 John 4:9-10)

Where Do You Live?

As a man thinks in his heart, so is he (Proverbs 23:7). Our mind set (what we think about) affects our actions, our attitudes, and our lifestyle. If we want to live in the Spirit, we must allow the Word of God and the power of the Holy Spirit to change how we think.

6. According to the following verses, on what are we to set our minds?
   a) Psalm 119:13-14
   b) Romans 8:5
   c) Philippians 4:8
   d) Colossians 3:2

7. Match the following Scripture references with what the Word says concerning the mind set of the believer.
   a. Isaiah 26:3
   b. Luke 10:27
   c. 1 Corinthians 2:16
   d. 2 Corinthians 10:5
   e. Philippians 2:3
   f. Philippians 4:6
   g. 2 Timothy 1:7
   h. Titus 2:6

   ____We have been given a sound mind.

   ____We have the mind (wisdom, maturity) of Christ.

   ____We are to be sober-minded or self-controlled.

   ____We should love the Lord our God with all our mind.

   ____We should take every thought captive to the knowledge of Christ.

   ____We should be like-minded or one in mind with the Holy Spirit, having the same love and purpose.

   ____We should not be worried or anxious about anything.

   ____We will have perfect peace as we keep our minds on God and trust in Him.

The Practice of Christian Living

It is humanly impossible to live the Christian life. But the Holy Spirit gives us the power to do it. The Holy Spirit changes us from the inside out. In addition to producing fruit, the Holy Spirit provides power to help us do God's will.

8. Read Galatians 5:16-22. Use these verses to answer the following questions.
   a) What is different about Christians who live by the power of the Holy Spirit?
   b) Can we follow the sinful nature and the Spirit at the same time?
   c) What are some of the physical activities or works which are produced in the lives of those who live according to the flesh?
   d) What are the nine spiritual qualities or the fruit that is produced in the lives of those who live according to the Spirit?

9. Match the following Scripture references to the tasks which the Holy Spirit performs in the life of the believer.
   a. Mark 13:11
   b. Romans 8:26
   c. 1 John 2:27
   d. 1 John 4:16
   ____He helps us love.
   ____He helps us witness for Christ and know what to say.
   ____He helps us pray.
   ____He teaches us all things.

The Privileges of Christian Living

As we surrender our lives completely to Christ and follow the principles of the Word of God and the leading of the Holy Spirit, we will experience the blessings of God.

10. Read Romans 8:1-27 a second time. What are some of the wonderful blessings that we receive as a result of living according to the Spirit?
    a) Verse 1
    b) Verse 2
    c) Verse 4
    d) Verse 6
    e) Verse 13
    f) Verse 14
    g) Verse 15
    h) Verse 16
    i) Verses 26 and 27

PERSONAL APPLICATION

1. Have you escaped condemnation by believing that Jesus Christ is the Son of God who has paid for your sins on the Cross?

2. Have you completely surrendered your life to God?

3. Do you maintain that vital link of communicating with God in prayer on a daily basis?

4. "Garbage in, garbage out" is a term used in computer programming. Do a mental check-up.
    a) What do you feed your mind (through books, TV programs, music, etc.)?

b) How often do you read and meditate on the Word of God?

c) During this past week, how often have you allowed your mind to be occupied with the following: a dishonest report; an unjust comment; current events and subjects which are dubious, unsavory, or which dishonor God?

5. Read Galatians 5:14-25. Do you have any personal characteristics or habits which are hindering your walk? If so, confess them to the Lord and ask for His forgiveness and help in overcoming them.

CHURCH MINISTRY APPLICATION

1. To be effective in ministry, the body of Christ must live in the power of the Holy Spirit. How can the Church help its members understand the importance of living in the Spirit?

2. Where we live spiritually becomes evident in our conduct, attitudes, and activities. How can the Church use this evidence to determine what classes, activities, or programs will meet the needs of the congregation?

3. We can face the challenges of tomorrow negatively or positively. With a negative attitude, we will surely face defeat. However, when we live according to the Spirit and obey the Word of God, we will be victorious. How can the Church be encouraged to develop a spiritual mind set?

Thou Shalt Love

Thou shalt love thy God. There must be for me a deep sense of relatedness to God. This relatedness is the way by which there shall open for me more and more springs of energy and power, which will enable me to thread life's mysteries with life's clue. It is this, and this alone, that will make it possible for me to stand anything that life can or may do to me. I shall not waste any effort in trying to reduce God to my particular logic. Here in the quietness, I shall give myself in love to God.

Thou shalt love thy neighbor. How I must seek ever the maintenance of the kind of relatedness to others that will feed the springs of kindness and sympathy in me! I shall study how I may be tender without being soft; gracious without being ingratiating; kind without being sentimental; and understanding without being judgmental. Here in the quietness, I shall give myself in love to my neighbors.

Thou shalt love Thyself. I must learn to love myself with detachment. I must have no attitude toward myself that contributes to my own delinquency. I shall study how so to love myself that, in my attitude toward myself, I shall be pleasing to God and face with confidence what He requires of me. Here in the quietness, I give myself over to the kind of self-regard that would make me whole and clean in my own sight and in the sight of God.

Thou shalt love
Thy God
Thy neighbor
Thyself[8]

—*Howard Thurman*

110

LIVE
TO LOVE

You've heard it—you may have even said it: "If you love me, you would...."

How should we show love? On Valentine's Day, we send cards, flowers, and candy. On Mother's Day, it's more cards, phone calls, and dinner out. On Christmas, we give presents. For children, we are told that love involves quality time. For couples, it is often shown by a romantic evening, the size of an engagement ring, or a sexual relationship.

These are demonstrations of natural love. But we, who are spiritual, must look beyond the natural. We need to know how to show what we have received—the awesome love of God.

God's love is uncompromising and unconditional. It never fails; it prevails in every generation, operates under every condition, and reaches out to everyone. God has demonstrated His love for us by sending His Son into the world to die for us, even while we disregarded His love and rebelled against His authority.

The human heart is changed by an encounter with the love of God. The loving, caring nature of the Gospel transforms us and causes us to love the One who first loved us. Then the Holy Spirit places the love of God in our hearts so that we may, in turn, demonstrate God's love to others.

Remember the song, "What the world needs now is

love, sweet love. It's the only thing that there's just too little of"? We must show God's love to everyone—friends, enemies, and neighbors. It means loving the unlovely, being at peace with the restless, helping the helpless, and giving guidance to those who have lost their direction. The love of God is the power that can change the world.

Live to Love

Mark 12:28-34

One of the teachers of the law came and heard them debating. Noticing that Jesus had given them a good answer, he asked him, "Of all the commandments, which is the most important?"

"The most important one," answered Jesus, "is this: 'Hear, O Israel, the Lord our God, the Lord is one. Love the Lord your God with all your heart and with all your soul and with all your mind and with all your strength.' The second is this: 'Love your neighbor as yourself.' There is no commandment greater than these."

"Well said, teacher," the man replied. "You are right in saying that God is one and there is no other but him. To love him with all your heart, with all your understanding and with all your strength, and to love your neighbor as yourself is more important than all burnt offerings and sacrifices."

When Jesus saw that he had answered wisely, he said to him, "You are not far from the kingdom of God." And from then on no one dared ask him any more questions.

The road to understanding our own spirituality is not often easy. There are always questions. Sometimes it seems like there are more questions than answers.

Jesus was asked the question, "Which of the command-ments is the greatest?" This was a good and honest inquiry. In other words, "What does God really want from us?" Have you ever asked yourself this question, or do you shy away from considering it at all?

Jesus answered the question by combining two Old Testament Scriptures: "Hear, O Israel: The Lord our God, the Lord is one. Love the Lord your God with all your heart and with all your soul and with all your strength" (Deuteronomy 6:4-5, NIV), and ". . . love your neighbor as yourself" (Leviticus 19:18, NIV). The combination of these Scriptures demonstrates the consistency and conti-nuity of God's love in action.

So, the summary of the Law, as Jesus put it, is love—love of God and love of neighbor. The height of spiritual-ity, therefore, is to live to love. Is this possible? Can we really achieve this level of spirituality? How do we go about it?

Loving the Lord
The greatest commandment is love. The love that God demands is the loving response of the whole human per-sonality. God demands everything—our all, or nothing at all. "All to Jesus I owe. I surrender all." Love is a total commitment.

However, too many of us put the Lord God on the periphery of our lives. Instead of one God, we have many gods—gods that claim our time, money, energy, and other resources. We say we love God, but our hearts are far from Him.

We have an "I/it" relationship with God, rather than an "I/Thou" relationship. When we think of God, is it only because of need or convenience. God becomes little more than an equation. Maybe we think of God in these terms because we are self-centered; we think of all our relationships in terms of what they can do for us, rather than what we can give. We need to think more about Who the Lord is, and what kind of relationship we have with Him.

It ought to be easy to love God because of His wonderful love for us. God has given us everything we are and everything we have. Loving God is a bargain. God makes it pleasant, wonderful, and enjoyable. God has reached out to us in pure love, in spite of ourselves. He sent Jesus Christ to die for us and to bring healing and wholeness to our broken lives.

Loving Your Neighbor

Because God loves us, loving others becomes easier—especially when we see how interdependent we are. Jesus said to His disciples, "I give you a new commandment, that you love one another. Just as I have loved you, you should also love one another" (John 13:34, NRSV).

There can be no real love without the expression of love. We must, as is said in business, "take a proactive approach" to love and loving. We cannot truly love another unless we love God, and we cannot show God's love unless we love ourselves and our neighbors.

Jesus was also asked, "And who is my neighbor?" (Luke 10:29). In response to this question, Jesus told the parable of the man who fell among thieves. The Good Samaritan was the one who saw the need and helped the man. He met his need in a way that shows us all what it really means to love our neighbors and ourselves.

We are all debtors in this life. We owe somebody for everything good that has happened to us. Somebody started schools and colleges; somebody discovered a cure for certain diseases; somebody died for freedom. We are deeply in debt. Somebody cared for us as an infant; somebody developed this country; somebody fought against slavery. We owe a debt that we can never repay. It is a debt of love. The most we can do is to try to give love in return.

Immortal Love

We are called to a life of love—a love which has been expressed in Jesus Christ. When we love, we benefit ourselves most of all. We are not simply a bag of chemicals. We are made for immortality, and love is our fulfillment. "We know that we have passed from death to life because we love one another" (1 John 3:14, NRSV).

The love of God is the strongest force in the universe. God's love is complete. It has already accomplished its end. We have access to God through His immortal love. God's love is continual. God demonstrates His love toward us each day. In sorrow, He gives joy. In confusion, He gives peace. What an amazing love this is! Thanks be to God for this unspeakable gift of love.

BIBLE STUDY APPLICATION

Receiving God's Love

Love is the greatest gift of all (1 Corinthians 13:13). Godly love or *agape* is an unselfish seeking of another's good without regard to their worthiness. God has made His gift of love available to all who will receive it.

1. Read John 3:16-17; Romans 5:8; and 1 John 4:9-10. Use these verses to answer the following questions.

a) Who did God love?
b) What did He do because of His love?
c) When we receive God's gift of love, what do we get?

2. Match the following Scripture references with the way that God's love was manifested in Jesus Christ.
   a. Luke 19:10
   b. Luke 23:34; 1 Peter 2:23
   c. John 10:11; 1 John 3:16
   d. John 16:7
   e. Galatians 1:4; Titus 2:14
   f. Hebrews 7:25
   g. Revelation 1:5

   _____Coming to seek the lost.
   _____Praying for His enemies.
   _____Sending the Holy Spirit.
   _____Dying for us.
   _____Interceding for us.
   _____Washing away our sins.
   _____Giving Himself for us.

Responding to God's Love

Knowing that God's love is unconditional frees us from trying to be perfect or trying to earn His love by our performance. Knowing that God's love is continual also frees us from the fear of losing it. However, this same knowledge creates in us a desire to please Him and to show Him that we love Him in return.

3. How can we show that we love God?
   a) Luke 6:46-49 and John 14:21
   b) John 15:9-10 and 1 John 2:5
   c) 1 John 5:1-3 and 2 John 5-6

4. Read 1 John 4:7-21. Use these verses to answer the following questions.
    a) Where does love come from? (vv. 7-8)
    b) How has God revealed His love to us? (vv. 9-10)
    c) If we love God, what will we do? (v. 11)
    d) If we love one another, what does it show? (vv. 12-16)
    e) Why has this love been given to us? (v. 17)
    f) What does love free us from? (v. 18)
    g) Why do we love? (v. 19)
    h) How can we tell whether our love is true? (vv. 20-21)

Demonstrating God's Love to Others

The highest expression of our spirituality is seen when we demonstrate the love of God. The love of God is not a feeling. It is not shown by an emotional or verbal commitment. God's love is demonstrated by action. "Let us not love in word or speech but in deed and in truth" (1 John 3:18, RSV).

5. Read John 13:34-35. Use these verses to answer the following questions.
    a) Whose example should we follow?
    b) How would you describe the way He loved?
    c) What is the result when we practice this kind of love?

6. Read 1 Corinthians 13:4-7. Use the following verses to determine how Christians should demonstrate God's love to others.
    a) Verse 4
    b) Verse 5

c) Verse 6
d) Verse 7

7. How are we able to love others with God's love? (Romans 5:5; Galatians 5:22)

8. Read Luke 6:27-36. Use these verses to answer the following questions.
   a) What should we do to our enemies?
   b) What should we do to those who curse us?
   c) What should we do to those who challenge us?
   d) What should we do to those who would defraud us?
   e) What should we do to those who beg from us?
   f) What should we do to those who would steal from us?
   g) If we do these things and expect nothing in return, what will we receive? (See also 1 Corinthians 3:13-14.)
   h) If we do these things, whose example are we following? (See also Ephesians 4:32–5:2.)

9. Read Romans 12:9-21. Match each verse with the characteristic of love that it describes. (Some verses may describe more than one characteristic.)
   a. Verse 9
   b. Verse 10
   c. Verse 11
   d. Verse 12
   e. Verse 13
   f. Verse 14
   g. Verse 15
   h. Verse 16
   i. Verse 17

j. Verse 18
k. Verse 19
l. Verse 20
m. Verse 21

____fervent
____sympathetic
____doing right
____forgiving
____sincere
____humble
____devoted
____helpful
____peaceful
____joyful in hope
____good
____generous
____kind
____respectful
____patient in affliction
____compassionate
____hospitable
____faithful in prayer

10. God hates sin but loves the sinner. Use the following
verses to identify what we should hate.

a) Hebrews 1:9
b) Romans 12:9
c) 1 John 2:15-17

PERSONAL APPLICATION

1. Is the Lord number one in your life?

2. Do people know that you love God because you obey His Word?

3. Can others tell that you are a Christian by the love that you show?

4. Read Luke 19:41-48. Using Jesus' example, how can you have the attitude of Christ toward your enemies?

5. Look at the characteristics of love listed in question 9. Rate yourself from one to ten (ten is the highest) on how often each facet of love is demonstrated in your life. Ask God to help you grow in the areas that you score the lowest.

CHURCH MINISTRY APPLICATION

1. How can the Church ensure that the love of God is proclaimed during worship services?

2. How can the members encourage each other to love God with all their hearts, souls, minds, and strength?

3. How can the Church encourage its members to demonstrate love to one another in practical ways?

Wrong Between
Me and Thee

The concern which I lay bare before God today is:

Whatever disaffection there is between me and those who are or have been very close to me—

I seek the cause or root of such disaffection and, with the illumination of the mind of God, to understand it.

I give myself to the scrutiny of God that, whatever there may be in me that is responsible for what has happened,

I will acknowledge.

Where I have wronged or given offense deliberately or without intention, I seek a face-to-face forgiveness.

Where I have been wronged or have taken offense deliberately or without intention, I seek a face-to-face forgiveness.

What I can undo I am willing to try; what I cannot undo, with that I seek to make my peace.

How to do these things, what techniques to use, with what spirit—for these I need and seek the wisdom and the strength of God.

Whatever disaffection there is between me and those who are or have been very close to me, I lay bare before God.[19]

—Howard Thurman

FORGIVING AND FORGIVEN

He woke up suddenly and looked at the empty pillow beside him, then he turned to check the clock. Four o'clock shone in bright red fluorescent color in the dark room. He had dreamed that she was beside him. As he lay back onto the pillow, his mind recalled happier times—a beautiful bride, a smiling groom, and a bright future filled with hope and potential. Now he could only wonder what their outcome would be.

If he didn't know the Lord, he would have given up long ago. Even with God, there were times when it hurt too much. "How long, Lord?" he prayed. And with effort, he forced himself to consider God's Word.

He thought about Hosea—a preacher married to a prostitute—and how God illustrated how much He loves us, even when we are unfaithful. He thought about how Jesus prayed that God would forgive others, even as He hung from the cross. Finally, he thought of how God had forgiven him, and how much God loved them both.

He shook his head, almost refusing to agree. "It's hard, Lord!" he admitted brokenly. Then came the gentle reminder that without Christ he could do nothing, but he could do all things through Christ who strengthened him (John 15:5; Philippians 4:13).

Each of us is in need of forgiveness, and we also have the need to forgive. What burdens we carry when we do not allow the forgiveness of God to work in and through our brokenness!

As we identify our pains and hurts, we can then offer them to God who will, in turn, heal us and others through us. In spite of what we may think of ourselves, none of us is perfect. We all are in need of someone to help us. Thank God we have an Advocate; we have someone who can plead our case before the throne of God. Jesus Christ intercedes on our behalf.

Some of us, because of our pride, will refuse to admit that there are areas in our lives which we have not yet brought before the living God—things we have not confessed or admitted that need to be touched in a specific way by the love of God. Nevertheless—no matter how else we may describe ourselves—we are a fellowship of forgiven people, saved from our guilt and stain by the grace of God.

The Fellowship of the Forgiven

1 John 2:1-6

My dear children, I write this to you so that you will not sin. But if anybody does sin, we have one who speaks to the Father in our defense—Jesus Christ, the Righteous One. He is the atoning sacrifice for our sins, and not only for ours but also for the sins of the whole world.

We know that we have come to know him if we obey his commands. The man who says, "I know him," but does not do what he commands is a liar, and the truth is not in him. But if anyone obeys his word, God's love is truly made complete in him. This is how we know we are in him: Whoever claims to live in him must walk as Jesus did.

The Christian Church has often been accused of fostering guilt and condemnation within people. Speaking objectively, there may be an element of truth in that accusation. Nevertheless, the New Testament makes it very clear that Jesus came into the world not to condemn it, but that the world through Him might be saved (John 3:17).

The world is in need of the Saviour. People's hurts need to be healed; people's pains need to be alleviated so that we might find rest in our weary souls. Some people suffer from guilt and a sense of loss in their lives. Others are uncomfortable with the word "sin." They would rather say "illness," "weakness," "failure," or "fault." However, if we are to be cured of our illnesses, then we must be aware of what those illnesses really are.

The Bible says that we are a sinful people. There are some who think that they are beyond being sinners. However, the truth is that we are all tempted to sin, and sin we will. The only way to a permanent solution is to recognize our need for help. Our help can come only from the Lord, who made the heavens and the earth. We must acknowledge that our very basic need is for God's love and forgiveness. We will find what we need in Jesus Christ.

God's Love and Forgiveness

How did it all happen? God gave us freedom. God gave us the power to choose, and we chose to sin. Our choices are acts of the will, and we have willfully chosen to act against God. The very first humans made a decision to disobey God's will, and we have been disobeying God's Word ever since. "Prone to wander. . . prone to leave the God I love." However, even in our disobedience and sin, God loves us.

God came after us to call us to repentance and renewal. Jesus came into the world to save us. We are called to *metanoia* which means "repentance, transformation." We are called to repentance and faith in Jesus Christ.

God guaranteed His love for us on Calvary. Christ's dying on the Cross for our sins was God's way of demonstrating—in absolute and unequivocal terms—His love for us. The Cross represents God at God's best and humanity at its worst. Were it not for the Cross, there would be no way out of our sinfulness. "Behold the Lamb of God, which taketh away the sin of the world" (John 1:29, KJV).

Forgiveness is part of God's plan of redemption. Forgiveness means "starting over; a clean slate; a new beginning." "So if anyone is in Christ, there is a new creation; everything old has passed away; see, everything has become new!" (2 Corinthians 5:17, NRSV) We are forgiven because Jesus Christ died on the Cross for our justification.

In faith we accept God's promise of eternal life in Jesus Christ. Then, by the power and presence of the Holy Spirit, God renews us inwardly so that we may be attuned to His will, direction, and purpose in our lives. With this acceptance and renewal we truly become a fellowship of God's forgiven people.

God's Forgiven People

God has arranged for us to be part of a community of people who have also been forgiven. As people who know God's love and forgiveness, we also need to love and forgive each other. This creates a new understanding of our relationship to others and God's intention of building the body of Christ on earth. "Thy will be done in earth, as it is in heaven" (Matthew 6:10b, KJV). This is part of God's new order—God's new design for us in Jesus Christ.

Forgiveness, therefore, has three parts:

1. God forgives all of our sins.
2. We can then forgive ourselves.
3. We then forgive each other.

As a forgiven people, we enter into the dynamics of a new relationship with others who are like-minded. We can also view relationships with others who may not be of the community of faith as opportunities to share how they, too, can be forgiven and can learn how to forgive.

We come to realize that learning how to forgive ourselves and, in turn, how to forgive others may be the key to developing our own inward spirituality. True spirituality begins with the knowledge that God has come to offer us forgiveness through Jesus Christ.

Our Assurance of Forgiveness

Just as we have received forgiveness through Christ's death on the Cross, we are empowered through the risen Christ. The Resurrection of Jesus Christ assures us that the love of God is certain and everlasting. The Saviour of the world is the risen Lord, who has conquered death, hell, and the grave. Because of the Resurrection, we have a sure and certain hope in Jesus Christ. The promises of God are true because Jesus Christ is alive. "Because I live," Jesus said, "ye shall live also" (John 14:19b, KJV). We have life, hope, joy, and peace—we are forgiven—because of Jesus Christ, the risen Saviour and Lord.

BIBLE STUDY APPLICATION

Receiving God's Forgiveness

God offers us forgiveness through Jesus Christ because He loves us. "This is love: not that we loved God, but that he loved us and sent his Son as an atoning sacrifice for our sins" (1 John 4:10, NIV).

1. Match the following verses with the characteristic of God's forgiveness that it describes.
   a. Psalm 78:38
   b. Psalm 103:12
   c. Psalm 130:4
   ____available
   ____compassionate
   ____complete

2. Why did Jesus come? (1 John 3:8; Colossians 1:19-22)

3. We can learn much from Jesus' ministry on earth. Use the verses from the Book of Luke and the related Scriptures to answer the following questions.
   a) Read Luke 3:3; 17:3; and Acts 3:18-19. What role does repentance play in receiving forgiveness?
   b) Read Luke 15:21-24; 18:13-14; and 1 John 1:9. What role does confession play in receiving forgiveness?
   c) Read Luke 5:20 and John 8:24. What role does faith play in receiving forgiveness?
   d) Read Luke 7:47 and 1 John 4:19. What should be our response when we are forgiven?

4. After we have received forgiveness through Jesus Christ, how can we keep our lives free from sin?
   a) Psalm 51:7-10
   b) Psalm 119:9, 11 and 2 Corinthians 7:1
   c) Philippians 1:10
   d) 1 John 3:2-3

Forgiven

There are many religious terms which are used to describe the forgiveness we have received from God through Jesus Christ. Let's make sure we know what the Bible says about what we speak and sing about.

5. We often sing about the blood, but do we really know why? Read Leviticus 17:11 and Hebrews 9:22. Use these verses to answer the following questions.
   a) What is the significance of the blood?
   b) What did the Law require?

6. Use the following verses to discuss the importance of the blood of Jesus.
   a) According to the prophesy in Matthew 1:21, who would save us from our sin?
   b) What did Jesus announce in Matthew 26:28?
   c) What did Jesus obtain for us? (Colossians 1:13-14)
   d) What did Jesus give in exchange? (Hebrews 9:12)
   e) Why is the blood important? (1 John 1:7)
   f) Why did Jesus do this for us? (Revelation 1:5)

7. We often talk about being redeemed, but do we know what it means? Use the following verses to discuss the

relationship between redemption and forgiveness.
   a) What does redemption mean? If we are redeemed, what should we do? (1 Corinthians 6:20; 7:23)
   b) Who was sent to redeem us? (Galatians 4:4-5)
   c) How did we receive redemption? (Ephesians 1:7; 1 Peter 1:18-19)

8. The Bible talks about a new covenant. Read Matthew 26:26-28; Hebrews 8:6; and 13:20. Use these verses to answer the following questions.
   a) How has our new covenant with God been established?
   b) How does the new covenant compare to the old?
   c) How long will the new covenant last?

Forgiving Others

We are a fellowship of sinners saved by the grace of God. As we allow the Holy Spirit to work in and through our lives, He will enable us to forgive others just as we have received forgiveness through Christ.

9. According to the following verses, why should we forgive?
   a) Matthew 6:12-15; Mark 11:25-26; Luke 6:37
   b) Ephesians 4:32; Colossians 3:13

10. Read Matthew 18:23-35 and Galatians 6:7. Use these verses to answer the following questions.
   a) Should there be a limit to our forgiveness?
   b) What kind of consequences are given for unforgiveness in this parable or illustration?
   c) Describe the relationship between giving and receiving forgiveness.

PERSONAL APPLICATION

1. Sin is still dangerous for believers. Why is obeying God important? (John 14:15; Romans 6:16)

2. Do you have a "pet" sin or an area that is especially hard for you to deal with? If so, take time to confess it and ask for God's help.

3. Christ died so that we could be forgiven. Is there someone you should forgive today as an act of gratitude to Christ?

4. What prevents you from forgiving others?

5. What can give you the strength to forgive the unforgivable?

CHURCH MINISTRY APPLICATION

1. How can the Church foster an attitude of forgiveness and inspire obedience to God's Word?

2. How can members be encouraged to follow Jesus' example in their relationships with others?

3. Can the Church improve its efforts to teach the meaning of the words that the congregation sings or hears during service?

I Surrender to God

To God I make a full surrender.

I SURRENDER to God the nerve center of my consent. This is the very core of my will, the mainspring of my desiring, the essence of my conscious thought.

I surrender to God the outlying districts of my self. These are the side streets down which I walk at night, the alleys of my desires, the parts of me that have not been laid out with streets, the wooded area, the swamps and marshlands of my character.

I surrender to God the things in my world to which I am related. These are the work I do, the things I own or that threaten me with their ownership, the points at which I carry social responsibility among my fellows, the money I earn, my delight in clothes and good food.

I surrender to God the hopes, dreams and desires of my heart. These are the things I reserve for my innermost communion; these are the fires that burn on the various altars of my life; these are the outreaches of my spirit enveloping all the hurt, the pain, the injustices and the cruelties of life. These are the things by which I live and carry on.

To God I make a full surrender this day.[20]

—*Howard Thurman*

CHAPTER TEN

COUNT
THE COST

Throughout history, Black men and women have given their lives so that we could be free. We know only a few of their names—people like Harriet Tubman, Medgar Evers, and Rev. Martin Luther King, Jr. Countless others fought to preserve the country and protect their families. Often, we remember them only by the names of their groups— brave soldiers like the Tuskegee Airmen, the 54th Massachusetts Infantry, and the Buffalo Soldiers. Many more of our forefathers and –mothers have sacrificed their lives for a cause that was bigger than themselves. They were willing to pay the price for freedom. They were willing to risk their own lives to preserve peace and protect others.

Sacrifice is, in fact, part and parcel of the human experience. Parents make sacrifices for their children. Some teachers make great sacrifices of their time to tutor, mentor, or counsel students. We are all, at some time in our lives, called upon to make a sacrifice of some kind.

There is a gospel being preached today which says that all is well with the world, regardless of what our senses and sensibilities tell us. "It is just a matter of faith," they say to us. The "gospel of prosperity" leaves out sacrifice and suffering. It feeds into the desires of this generation, which wants to have it all—everything—and wants to give up nothing.

We are not used to giving up anything. People today look around at others and think, "I have mine, now you get yours the best way you can." However, the old saying is still true: "You can't get something for nothing." To get something, you have to give up something.

God has already made the supreme sacrifice for us. God sent His only Son to die so that our relationship with Him might be restored. Salvation is free because Jesus paid the price for us by His death on the Cross. Now, we who have received the awesome gift of God's grace must be willing to give our lives to God in return.

The Christian life calls us to a new level and dimension of living. Our spirituality, as defined by Jesus Christ, is much more than noise and emotion. It is, in fact, the best example of sacrifice in action. For the Christian, this sacrifice means that we give up and give in to the divine initiative.

As we die to ourselves and give our lives completely to the God who made us, the true essence of who we are will be demonstrated. God does have a plan. If we make the sacrifice, God provides abundant and everlasting life.

The Price of Spirituality

Mark 8:34-38

Then he called the crowd to him along with his disciples and said: "If anyone would come after me, he must deny himself and take up his cross and follow me. For whoever wants to save his life will lose it, but whoever loses his life for me and for the gospel will save it. What good is it for a man to gain the whole world, yet forfeit his soul? Or what can a man give in exchange for his soul? If anyone is ashamed of me and of my words in this adulterous and sinful generation, the Son of Man will be ashamed of him when he comes in his Father's glory with the holy angels."

As we journey along, we have discovered that spirituality is the expression of who we are in relationship to Jesus Christ, the Church, the community, and the world. Real spirituality is the highest quality of life. It is available to all, but it is not cheap. What does it cost, really?

In the book, *The Cost of Discipleship,* Dietrich Bonhoeffer speaks of cheap grace and costly grace.[21] Cheap grace is grace which does not make any demands on the lives of those who receive it. It allows God's people to live as helter-skelter, in-and-out, now-and-then Christians. When grace is cheap, we can live on the fringes of the fellowship of Christ—never really in, just around.

However, Mark 8:34-38 indicates very strongly that Jesus calls us to be His disciples. Discipleship denotes sacrifice and commitment. It costs to be a disciple. If we are called to be disciples, we are called to costly grace. In this text, Jesus spells out the price of real spirituality. He told those who would be His disciples that in order to do so, they would need to deny themselves, take up the cross, and follow Him (v. 34).

Denying Yourself
Denying yourself is different from self-denial. Self-denial has to do with giving up things—such as chewing

gum, high cholesterol foods, or stressful activities. Denying yourself means that you relinquish the right to your own life. It means turning your life over to the will and direction of Christ.

Giving up self-interest is not very easy because we are taught to think of ourselves first. The first law of preservation is "self." Denying yourself requires a change in attitude. It means giving up self-centeredness and selfishness—the "me, myself, and I" attitude. It means a change in disposition toward yourself and others.

Denying yourself also involves service. It means following the example of our Lord, who came not to be served but to serve (Matthew 20:28).

Taking Up the Cross

The cross is the symbol of suffering and death. Everyone has a cross. In this country, the African American community especially has a cross to bear—a cross fashioned from racism, bigotry, and discrimination from the outside; and violence, violent death, and drugs from the inside. The crosses of life can be heavy burdens for people who are trying to live decently and with dignity.

However, the cross also speaks to the sin and selfishness of our lives. Jesus' Cross was the payment for our sinfulness—He conquered death, hell, and the grave so that we could have life. The Christian is identified with Christ in His suffering and death. As Christians who stand for Christ, we also have a cross to bear. "If the world hates you, keep in mind that it hated me first," Jesus told His disciples (John 15:18).

Death is the other aspect of bearing the cross. The cross means that we die to ourselves—the self that would cause us to be disobedient to the will of God. "I have been crucified with Christ," the Apostle Paul said (Galatians 2:20). "The world is crucified unto me, and I unto the world," he said again (Galatians 6:14, KJV).

No death, no life; no cross, no crown. We must die to ourselves so that we can, without reservation, follow Christ.

Following Jesus

"Follow Me," Jesus says. Follow Jesus. Where?

We follow Him to Gethsemane, to Calvary, and to Easter morning's victory. We follow Him through our times of trial and testing, through times of doubt and questioning. However, even as we follow Him, we wonder sometimes about our willingness always to obey the voice of God and do what is right in His sight. We do not wish to drink from the cup of sorrow from which Jesus drank. Nevertheless, when we lose ourselves in the will of God, we are spiritually enabled to echo the voice of Jesus and say, in prayerful resignation, "Thy will be done."

We will follow Jesus. We will follow Jesus to Calvary, even into the valley of the shadow of death. We will follow Him through the darkness of the grave into the light of the Resurrection. We will follow Him into new life, hope, joy, and peace. We will follow Him into sacrifice and fulfillment. We will follow Him all the way, even unto that day when we hear the voice of our God say, "Well done, good and faithful servant" (Matthew 25:23).

Finding Life

To keep our spiritual commitment, we must consider the question: "What will it profit a person to gain everything this world has and lose his or her own soul?" (Matthew 16:26, NRSV) What will you receive in

137

exchange for your life, for your character, for your integrity, for your freedom to be what God has called you to be?

The enticement is everywhere: "Sell out yourself, if you will. Sell your integrity; sell your character; sell your honesty; sell out your community in order to get ahead, if you will." And, there are too many people who are willing to give up everything—people who are straining for a bigger piece of the American pie, and they are choking on it . . . choking to death.

For both Christians and non-Christians, Christ's values and Christ's way of life are being left out of everyday living. We leave Christ out of our businesses, out of our homes, out of our communities and social activities, only to end up in existential hell.

We are too caught up in this world. We are concerned with what we do—our titles, when we should be defined by who we are. We are surrounded by people who have all the credentials but no character, no integrity, and no other purpose in life than to fulfill their own selfish desires.

However, Jesus instructs His disciples that to find one's life, one must lose it (Matthew 10:39). True life is found in Jesus Christ. Life is not found in possessions acquired by our own hands, nor in what we do or cannot do. But life with a capital "L"—abundant and everlasting life—is found in Jesus Christ who said, "I am the way, the truth, and the life" (John 14:6, KJV).

Not Ashamed

Just as Jesus called to the crowd in Mark 8:34, He calls each of us to Himself today. We are called into a relationship with Jesus Christ by the conviction of the Holy Spirit, and by the power of the Holy Spirit we are transformed and renewed day by day into the image of Jesus Christ.

An acorn cannot grow into an oak until it dies to itself—gives up its own life. Similarly, we cannot grow spiritually until we die to self and follow Jesus in the paths of righteousness. Jesus said, "Abide in me as I abide in you. Just as the branch cannot bear fruit by itself unless it abides in the vine, neither can you unless you abide in me. I am the vine, you are the branches. Those who abide in me and I in them bear much fruit, because apart from me you can do nothing" (John 15:4-5, NRSV).

How can we be ashamed of the one who gave His life that we might have life? How can we be ashamed of Him who has given us hope, purpose, meaning, and direction? How can we be ashamed of Him who has freed us to be more than we could ever be?

When we give up our lives to live in Christ, we are fulfilling our highest and ultimate goal—to be all God has called us to be. The cost of spirituality is an ever-widening, ever-deepening commitment to follow the abiding presence of the Holy Spirit in our lives as believers. The essence of spirituality is the knowledge that there is nothing more real, more substantial, or more valuable than our new life in Jesus Christ.

BIBLE STUDY APPLICATION

Becoming Christ's Disciples

Next to His redemptive work on the Cross, Jesus' most important ministry on earth was calling a group of willing and dedicated disciples who would impact the world.

Jesus ministered to the crowds because of His love and compassion. But God cannot use people who will follow Him only for the benefits. The Word of God says, "Jesus

Christ is the same yesterday and today and forever" (Hebrews 13:8, NRSV). Jesus is calling committed followers who have counted the cost and upon whom He can depend.

1. Use the following verses to identify how discipleship affects our **minds.**
   Count the cost:
   > a) Matthew 22:37
   > b) Romans 12:2; Ephesians 4:23
   > c) 2 Corinthians 10:5

   Identify the benefits:
   > d) 1 Corinthians 2:16
   > e) 2 Timothy 1:7
   > f) Hebrews 8:10

2. Use the following verses to identify how discipleship affects our **bodies.**
   Count the cost:
   > a) Romans 12:1
   > b) 1 Corinthians 6:19-20
   > c) 1 Corinthians 9:27

   Consider Jesus' example:
   > d) Matthew 26:26-28:
   > e) 1 Peter 2:24

   Identify the benefits:
   > f) Romans 6:6
   > g) Romans 8:13
   > h) Philippians 3:21

3. Use the following verses to identify how discipleship affects our **goals** and **pursuits.**
   Count the cost:

    a) Matthew 6:19-21
    b) Matthew 6:24
    c) Matthew 6:33
    d) Colossians 3:1-3
    e) Romans 14:19; 1 Peter 3:11
    f) 1 John 2:15-17
Consider Jesus' example:
    g) John 5:30
Identify the benefits:
    h) Matthew 7:7
    i) Hebrews 11:6
    j) Hebrews 13:5

4. Use the following verses to identify how discipleship affects our service.
Count the cost:
    a) Ephesians 6:6
    b) Colossians 3:17, 23-24
    c) John 12:26
Consider Jesus' example:
    d) John 9:4
    e) Philippians 2:3-11
Identify the benefits:
    f) John 12:26
    g) Romans 2:6; 2 Corinthians 5:10
    h) Hebrews 6:10
    i) James 1:25

5. Use the following verses to identify how discipleship affects our **will**.
Count the cost:
    a) Proverbs 3:5-6
    b) John 14:21

Consider Jesus' example:
    c) Matthew 26:39
    d) Luke 11:2
    e) John 6:38
Identify the benefits:
    f) Matthew 7:21
    g) Matthew 12:50
    h) John 14:21

6. Use the following verses to identify how discipleship affects our **attitudes**.
Count the cost:
    a) Philippians 4:11
    b) Colossians 3:8-9
    c) Colossians 3:12-17
Consider Jesus' example:
    d) Matthew 11:29
    e) Matthew 14:14; Mark 6:34
    f) Philippians 2:5-11
Identify the benefits:
    g) Matthew 5:3-12
    h) Galatians 5:22-23
    i) 1 Timothy 6:6-7
    j) 1 Peter 3:4

7. Use the following verses to identify how discipleship affects our **relationships**.
Count the cost:
    a) Matthew 10:37; Luke 9:59-62
Consider Jesus' example:
    b) Matthew 12:46-50
Identify the benefits:
    c) Matthew 19:29

8. Use the following verses to identify how discipleship affects our **conversation**.
   Count the cost:
   - a) Matthew 12:36
   - b) Luke 6:45
   - c) John 7:18
   - d) Ephesians 4:15
   - e) Ephesians 6:20; 1 Thessalonians 2:4
   - f) 1 Peter 3:9-10; Titus 3:2
   - g) 1 Peter 3:15-16
   - h) James 1:19; 26

   Consider Jesus' example:
   - i) John 6:63
   - j) John 12:49; 14:10

   Identify the benefits:
   - k) Proverbs 18:21
   - l) 1 Peter 3:10:

PERSONAL APPLICATION

1. Have you decided to follow Christ?

2. Have you considered the cost of discipleship in your love life? Your dating conduct? Your family relationships? Your friendships? Your career or vocation? Your finances? Your future plans?

3. Why do you think we must be willing to give up everything to follow Christ? (Luke 14:25-33)

4. We often give God the leftovers of our life when we should be giving Him our all and our best. What kind of excuses keep you from following Christ wholeheartedly?

5. Have you ever seriously considered the benefits of discipleship and the price that Jesus paid for you?

CHURCH MINISTRY APPLICATION

1. How can the Church help the congregation understand the cost and the benefits of following Christ?

2. How can the Word of God be used to encourage the members to follow Jesus despite persecution or suffering?

3. What kind of programs, activities, or opportunities can the Church provide to encourage members to demonstrate their discipleship in practical ways?

O God of Love, Power and Justice
(1990)

O God of love, Power and Justice, who wills the freedom and fulfillment of all your children. We thank you for the constancy of your loving kindness and tender mercies toward us. Especially on this day as we celebrate the birthday and life of your servant and prophet, Dr. Martin Luther King, Jr. We are reminded that in every age you raise up seers and sayers and doers of justice.

Because our needs are so great today, and your care so constant, we know that you are rebuilding the network of compassion around new visionaries whom you have assembled for this hour. Surprise us with the discovery of how much power we have to make a difference in our day:

— A difference in the way citizens meet, greet, respect, and protect the rights of each other.

— A difference in the breadth of our vision of what is possible in humanization, reconciliation, and equalization of results in our great city.

— A difference in the way government, business, and labor can work together, for justice and social enrichment.

— A difference in our response to the needy, and a difference in our appreciation for those who give of themselves for the surviving and thriving of our beautiful people.

Use this season of celebration to spark new hope and stir up our passion for new possibilities. Make compassion and the spirit of sacrifice to be the new mark of affluence of character. Strengthen us to face reality and to withstand the rigor of tough times in the anticipation of a bright side beyond the struggle. Inspire, empower, and sustain us until we reach the mountaintop, and see that future for which our hearts yearn.

This is our fervent and sincere prayer. Amen.[22]

—*James Alexander Forbes, Jr.*

CHAPTER ELEVEN

OPEN FOR BUSINESS

Everyone has a job to do. Even students have homework, the employed must work to make ends meet, and those who are homeless work every day just to stay alive. The Bible has a lot to say about the importance of work. In the Genesis account of creation, we saw God at work. When God created Adam, He gave him the job of "tending" the Garden of Eden (Genesis 2:15). In the Gospels, we saw the work of Jesus Christ. Jesus sent forth His disciples to become laborers in God's harvest (Luke 10:2-3). We were made to work. It's part of our God-given ability and talent.

As Christians, our most important work is spiritual. When we speak of spirituality, we are talking about God's abiding presence in the life of the Church and in the life of the believer. However, spirituality and social reality cannot be separated. More than ever before, the spotlight is on the Church to demonstrate our spirituality in ways that the world can see and understand. We must connect the spiritual with the physical and the material. Faith without works is dead (James 2:17). Our inward faith must be demonstrated by outward manifestations.

All around us we see that people are suffering. There are deep hurts and wounds in people's lives. We must reach out to them in love and concern. This is the calling of God to us. Our business is people. Through the presence of the Holy Spirit, we are empowered to do the work and will of God on earth. "For we are God's workmanship, created in Christ Jesus to do good works, which God prepared in advance for us to do" (Ephesians 2:10, NIV).

The Business of Spirituality

Acts 3:1-10

One day Peter and John were going up to the temple at the time of prayer—at three in the afternoon. Now a man crippled from birth was being carried to the temple gate called Beautiful, where he was put every day to beg from those going into the temple courts. When he saw Peter and John about to enter, he asked them for money. Peter looked straight at him, as did John. Then Peter said, "Look at us!" So the man gave them his attention, expecting to get something from them.

Then Peter said, "Silver or gold I do not have, but what I have I give you. In the name of Jesus Christ of Nazareth, walk." Taking him by the right hand, he helped him up, and instantly the man's feet and ankles became strong. He jumped to his feet and began to walk. Then he went with them into the temple courts, walking and jumping, and praising God. When all the people saw him walking and praising God, they recognized him as the same man who used to sit begging at the temple gate called Beautiful, and they were filled with wonder and amazement at what had happened to him.

We are at a critical point in history. The world lies at our doorstep. The world is paralyzed with racism, sexism, and classism. The world is crippled by bigotry, prejudice, greed, selfishness, and the lust for power. Even the Church has been crippled by jealousy, envy, strife, heresy, gossip, and anger.

We live in a time that demands that our faith be actualized in our behavior. We can no longer ignore what we see and hear. We cannot afford to ignore the condition of the world around us. How do we address these conditions? "What can we do?" is always the question. We search for the answers to the problems which always seem to be with us. We have tried various means.

Some have said that education is the answer. No doubt education has helped to advance our society.

Others have said that economics is the answer. Very well; a little money has helped some people succeed. However, money has not solved the problems of human relationships. In fact, it seems to a large degree that in our country wealth has helped to create a larger underclass of people.

"Religion is the answer," some declare. We have enough religions to make every man and woman, boy and girl more than moral. However, it will take more than religion to make people into what they ought to be.

"Politics is the answer," others will declare. Get people politically involved and then you will see change. Politics has its place, and as a people we need to become more involved in the political arena of our community. However, political involvement will not guarantee a better community and world.

Then what, one may ask, will help transform us and our communities into what they ought to be? The Bible gives us the answer.

The Book of Acts, chapter 3 tells the story of two people whose lives had been transformed by the power and love of Jesus Christ. Peter and John were two contrasting personalities in the New Testament. Peter was outspoken and impulsive, while John was reflective and quiet. However, here they are together going into the temple to pray.

Peter and John were practicing their spirituality. Following the custom of the day, they were going into the temple, the central place of worship, in order to have their spiritual lives renewed through their prayers to the living God. Peter and John were fully cognizant of the need for spiritual empowerment.

The Power of Prayer

Spiritual power must come from a spiritual connection with the source of power, which is in God the Holy Spirit. It is through prayer that our spirits interact with the Spirit of the living God. Based on this interaction we are then able to put our prayers into action.

Peter and John were connected to the source of power, which gave them the power to heal the man at the gate of the temple. Prayer was then, and is now, true communication with the living God. It was because the early Christian Church prayed that they were able to transform their world. Answered prayer produces power in the life of the Church.

When will we learn that prayer is the key to divine power, healing, growth, and direction in the name of Jesus Christ? Jesus knew the importance of praying. The early Christian disciples knew it. When will Christians of the 20th century learn?

What Do We Have to Offer?

Peter and John said, "Look at us!" (Acts 3:4) When we go to the world, we should get the world's attention. Why should the world look at us? What do we have to offer?

We make the mistake of offering people the wrong things. We say to them, "Look, come to our church; look at our programs; look how lovely our building looks." We are offering the wrong things. We need to offer people more than we have been offering. Instead of giving love to our children, we give them things. Instead of giving them advice, we let them go with whoever comes along. Instead of telling them that they ought to keep themselves for marriage, we offer them aids to protect themselves. Instead of offering hope to the hopeless, instead of offering peace to the confused, instead of offering love to the angry, instead of offering healing to the broken, we have offered insubstantial, temporary remedies.

If we don't have anything, we can't give anything. We can only offer what we have. As people who have been redeemed by the blood of Jesus Christ, we understand what it means to have someone reach out in love and concern. Jesus was moved with compassion. He saw human need and sought to meet it in the name of the Lord. Like our Lord and Saviour, we too must have compassion for the multitude.

The Bible teaches us that if we love God, we should love our sisters and brothers, as well. Love is not only spoken, it is also shown by our behavior. We who are the people of God need to reach out to those whose lives are broken, hopeless, and aimless. We offer Jesus Christ to a crippled world, paralyzed and broken, because we ourselves know and are known by Him.

To the world, we say, "Take Jesus. Jesus Christ and Jesus alone is able to meet your every need. Take the hand of Jesus and He will strengthen you."

Demonstrating Our Spirituality

Spirituality is demonstrated through the meeting of human needs and the relieving of human suffering. Humanity's needs can and must be met through the people of Jesus Christ. The lame man at the gate of the temple represents the world at the doorstep of the Church. He represents humanity at large, with all its needs. He was accustomed to begging until Peter and John came along and changed the course of his life.

Peter and John were people of spiritual action because they had met the Saviour, who had sent them into the world to continue His ministry, touching especially the lives of those who were in need. This is the challenge we face today. Spirituality does not mean self-containment; it means going where people are in need and ministering to those needs through the power of the Holy Spirit.

God is able to heal all manner of diseases—diseases of the body, the mind, and the heart. What does God's power and love do for our crippled world? The man at the gate had become adjusted to his condition; he needed to be freed from his circumstances. There are people who are bound to bad habits, a distorted view of life, a lack of self-awareness and the inability to see their own potential. The power of God sets us free from bondage, whatever the source may be. The love of God gives us new self-awareness, a new sense of dignity. God's love helps us stand taller, with self-assurance.

The man so blessed by Peter and John received strength in his legs and he got up. He arose to a new life in Jesus Christ. He had never walked before. He had been battered, bruised, and beaten down by life's circumstances. Now a change had come. The Bible says he leaped up, walking and running into the temple.

He didn't go back home (if he had one); he didn't go to the local lounge to have a drink or take some drugs. He went into the temple. He probably had wanted to go into it before, but no one had taken him in; no one had invited him to come in. They left him on the outside, at the gate. Now he could go in.

The man ran into the temple, walking, leaping, and praising God. What has the Lord done in your life? If the Lord has done anything in your life, you ought to praise Him. If He has done something new and wonderful in your life, tell it; shout it; proclaim it. Let people know of God's goodness, greatness, and grace in your life.

Somebody is waiting for you to bring him or her into the temple. The temple is the symbol of God's presence. Somebody is waiting for your invitation to come into the presence of a loving, healing, forgiving, delivering God.

Spiritual Enterprise

We are empowered to do the work of God through the Holy Spirit Who abides in us. The Spirit of God infuses us with the power to walk, run, and even leap into new areas of service to humankind. The power of God releases us from greed, selfishness, and bigotry to the freedom found in a life of giving, love, and openness to others.

Jesus told His disciples that He had come to do the will of His Father, who had sent Him (John 14:24). The will of God had to be demonstrated. Jesus went about doing good. He healed the sick, gave sight to the blind, healed the lepers, and fed the hungry. Jesus knew that the all but incomprehensible vastness of God's love had to be demonstrated before we could even begin to grasp its meaning and significance in our lives.

Our business, as the people of God, is to demonstrate the power and love of God that has been given to us in Jesus Christ. Our business is to do the work of Jesus—to do what Jesus did while He lived on earth. The evidence of our spirituality is marked by what we do for other people in the name of our Lord. People will know that we are God's people only by our expression of God's love.

Our inheritance of eternal life is based on a faith which produces good works. Our faith is shown through the works we do. These works, in turn, transform human lives and human circumstances through the power and presence of the Holy Spirit.

The business of spirituality, then, is feeding the hungry, clothing the naked, housing the homeless, visiting the sick, visiting the prisons, relieving human suffering, and meeting human needs. This is God's way, and it should be our way, too.

BIBLE STUDY APPLICATION

The Work of Jesus Christ
1. Use the following verses to examine the ministry of Jesus Christ.
> a) What work did Jesus come to finish? (John 4:34; 5:17, 36; 17:4)
> b) Describe the relationship between the works of Jesus and the identity of Jesus Christ. (John 10:37-38)
> c) What kind of works did Jesus do while on earth? (Matthew 9:35; Luke 4:18; Acts 10:38)
> d) Although Jesus was God's Son, He was also human. Who empowered Jesus to do the work? (John 14:10-11)

2. Use the following verses to describe how we should relate Jesus' example to our own spiritual work.
   a) Describe the relationship between our works and our identity as the children of God. (1 John 3:10; 5:2)
   b) What kind of work will we do and why? (John 14:12)
   c) What is the first step we must take if we are to do the work of God? (John 6:29)
   d) Who empowers us to perform our spiritual work? (Acts 1:8)

Prepared for Business
3. Use the following verses to identify how we can become prepared for spiritual business.
   a) Joshua 1:8; 2 Timothy 3:16-17
   b) Philippians 4:6-7; James 5:15-16
   c) John 14:21; 1 John 3:22-24
   d) 2 Timothy 2:20-21; James 4:7

4. Use the following verses to identify how the Holy Spirit prepares us for spiritual business.
   a) Revelation 22:17
   b) John 14:16
   c) John 14:26
   d) John 16:13-15
   e) Romans 8:26-27

The Nature of Our Business
5. Match the following verses with the terms that describe how spirituality affects our human relationships.
   a. Matthew 5:38-42
   b. Matthew 5:43-45
   c. Matthew 22:39
   d. John 13:34-35

e. Romans 12:3

f. 1 Peter 2:17

g. 1 Peter 4:10

_____We should love our enemies.

_____We should forgive our debtors and enemies.

_____We should serve others.

_____We should love our neighbors as ourselves.

_____We should consider others better than our-
selves.

_____We should love other believers.

_____We should show respect to every person
regardless of status.

6. Match the following verses with the terms that describe
the attitude that we should possess as we work.

a. 1 Corinthians 15:58

b. Ephesians 6:6-8

c. Titus 2:14

d. 1 Timothy 6:18

e. Colossians 3:17, 23-24

f. James 3:13

g. Titus 3:8

h. Titus 3:1

_____Steadfast and productive

_____Thankful

_____Zealous

_____Generous

_____Wholehearted

_____Done in meekness

_____Careful

_____Ready

The Rewards of Our Labor

7. Use the following verses to identify the purpose of spiritual work.
   a) Luke 10:2; James 5:20
   b) Romans 12:11; Ephesians 6:6
   c) Philippians 2:13; Colossians 1:10
   d) Matthew 5:16; 1 Peter 2:12
   e) 1 Peter 2:15; Hebrews 13:21
   f) John 3:21; Ephesians 3:20

8. Use the following verses to identify the rewards that the Lord will provide for His workers.
   a) John 12:26
   b) Romans 2:6; 2 Corinthians 5:10
   c) Ephesians 6:8
   d) Hebrews 6:10
   e) James 1:25
   f) 1 John 2:17

Quality Control

9. Read 1 Corinthians 3:10-15. Use these verses to answer the following questions.
   a) Who is our foundation?
   b) What will be tested?
   c) Who will be rewarded?
   d) Who will suffer loss?

10. Believers will not be judged for sin; Christ received this judgment. According to the following verses, for what will we be judged or give an account?
    a) Romans 14:12; 2 Corinthians 5:10
    b) Matthew 12:35-37

PERSONAL APPLICATION

1. Describe the relationship between your spiritual work and your faith in Jesus Christ.

2. How prepared are you? Evaluate the time you regularly spend in prayer and in reading the Word of God.

3. How well do you demonstrate your spirituality in your relationships with others? For example, how do you handle conflicts with "coworkers?" Does it make a difference if the conflict is with a Christian or a non-Christian? What does the Holy Spirit prompt you to do?

4. Do you regularly participate in activities which support the community? Help the poor? Spread the Gospel of Jesus Christ? Build up the body of Christ?

5. Evaluate the quality of your spiritual work. Are you offering God your best?

CHURCH MINISTRY APPLICATION

1. How can the Church help congregations understand that spiritual work is the job of every believer?

2. What kind of programs, activities, or opportunities can the Church provide to encourage members to prepare for and participate in spiritual work?

3. In what practical ways can the Church discourage competition and comparison and emphasize that the Lord alone judges and gives the rewards?

A Prayer before the
Everlasting Fountain
(1980)

Our Father and our God, we open now our very souls before Thee, for something within us craves food which the bread of this world cannot satisfy. We should slake our thirst at the everlasting fountain.

We thank Thee for all Thou hast done for us, for the way Thou hast shepherded us and provided for us all this journey through, for family and friends and the fulfillment of daily work. Above all, for Jesus Thy Son, our Lord.

We lift before Thee our nation, so splendid in possibility, so stricken and uncertain in this moment of its history. Give us again the vision of a nation under God, moving to be what Thou wouldest have us be and to do what Thou dost bid us do. We pray for all political prisoners and, indeed, for all who languish in cells anywhere. Likewise we hold up before Thee those who have come within sight of the grave. Sustain them. Bless our young people seeking to find the point and purpose of their lives. Bless all who are here and those who worship with us beyond this visible company.

Bless this Church and Thy churches everywhere. Put on Thy churches' lips the old Gospel of Bethlehem and Galilee and Calvary's resurrection morning. Come Thou among us. Set the fires of God burning afresh in our hearts.

Let the words we utter here with our mouths and the thoughts we think with our hearts, be acceptable in Thy sight, O Lord our strength and our Redeemer.

Through Jesus Christ our Lord we make our petition—Amen.[23]

—*Gardner Calvin Taylor*

TWELVE

SPIRITUAL RENEWAL

How do you see the world? It was Robert Kennedy who said, "Some people look at the world and ask, 'Why?' I look at the world and ask, 'Why not?'"

Why can't we make things different? Why don't we love one another? Why can't we act better? It's the question that Rodney King asked, "Why can't we get along?" That's it. Why can't we?

We need a new perspective. We must begin to see the world as God sees it, so that we can participate in His plan. We must develop spiritual vision, and we must become spiritually renewed.

A New Agenda

Revelation 21:1-5

Then I saw a new heaven and a new earth, for the first heaven and the first earth had passed away, and there was no longer any sea. I saw the Holy City, the new Jerusalem, coming down out of heaven from God, prepared as a bride beautifully dressed for her husband. And I heard a loud voice from the throne saying, "Now the dwelling of God is with men, and he will live with them. They will be his people, and God himself will be with them and be their God. He will wipe every tear from their eyes. There will be no more death or mourning or crying or pain, for the old order of things has passed away."

He who was seated on the throne said, "I am making everything new!" Then he said, "Write this down, for these words are trustworthy and true."

Our agenda is first of all to see the vision that God has for the world. The vision is quite clear in the Book of Revelation. John saw a new world, a new universe, a new order, and a new reality. Words cannot describe the reality. The words are just words, and therefore only symbols. The reality is beyond description. But John does say, "I saw it." He saw the vision.

We must become spiritually renewed. When will we become tired of thinking the same old way? Tired of all these negative, oppressive thoughts running through our minds. Tired of allowing our minds to be filled with garbage.

When will we become tired of talking about the same

old stuff? Tired of speaking unkind words which hurt others. Tired of being negative and critical all the time. Tired of gossiping and backbiting.

When will we become tired of behaving the same old way? Tired of doing the same old things, over and over again. Tired of being selfish. Tired of being mean and tired of being greedy. Tired of being self-centered. When will we become burdened by our own behavior and want to change? Really want our hearts to change so our behavior can change.

People often say, "Well, I've been trying to change my life. I've been making New Year's resolutions every year." But before the first day of the New Year ends, they've broken most of them. That's what happened when the Apostle Paul said, "When I try to do good, evil is present with me" (Romans 7:21, paraphrased).

We can't even help ourselves. We need somebody who can really help. There is Someone who knows us—Someone who can help us with our dilemma. God can heal the wounds of our hearts and bring deliverance to our bodies. God can put new thoughts in our minds and give us a new heart.

Candidates for Renewal

To become candidates for spiritual renewal, we must first decide to trash it. We have to say, "Lord, I quit. I give up. I surrender. I can't do this myself, Lord. I need Your help! Empty my mind of garbage and fill it with the thoughts of God. Put new words in my mouth—words of kindness, encouragement, hope, and love." When will we say, "Lord, I want to become new"?

God has already given us the answer. Throughout the Word, God says, "I will help you. I will give you the strength you need. You can be that person that you want to be in your heart. You can learn to speak words which uplift, encourage, and give hope. You can behave in a new way. You can become a new person. I will change you. I will change your character" (Psalm 19:14; Isaiah 41:10; Ephesians 4:24, paraphrased). "For," God says, "I am making all things new!" (Revelation 21:5, paraphrased).

In order to have new things, you have to have new people. That's why Jesus came—to create a new people. "Therefore, if anyone is in Christ, he is a new creation; the old has gone, the new has come!" (2 Corinthians 5:17, NIV)

Our God is in the process of making a new people. It's happening already. You may not see it, but it's happening. Every day somebody is coming to Jesus Christ. Every day somewhere a drug addict is being delivered from that drug. Every day an alcoholic is being delivered from alcohol. Every day a prostitute is being delivered from prostitution. Every day a person who was an abuser has stopped abusing, because Jesus Christ is making them new. It is happening every day.

Developing Spiritual Vision

Do you see a new world coming? Do you see yourself involved in making the world new? Are you making your community a better place to live, and thereby making this country a better nation and the world a better place?

It's not a Sunday morning thing. You see, here is the question we must ask ourselves, my sisters and my brothers, "Is God on the agenda at all?" I mean, if someone looked at your agenda, would they see God there? Would they see the church there? Would they see the Sunday School there? Would they see the Bible study on it? Do you have time for anything else? Do you have time for

God? Do you have time to nourish your spirit so you can be about the work which God has called us to do?

John saw a new heaven and earth. We must not only see the vision, we must become a part of it. We can't be on the outside; we can't be too busy. We must become a part of what God is doing in the world.

Like John, we will see that new heaven and earth as we seek the Lord. We will see a new community which includes boys and girls who are not shooting each other down in the streets. We will see people who are free from drugs and alcohol. We will see burdens lifted and heartaches healed. That's what spiritual renewal is all about. It's all a part of God's agenda.

No More Tears

Even as we see the vision becoming reality, we may still carry some of the same hurts and pain with us. We may have to face things that we do not particularly care to face. Yes, sometimes we have to cry. There will be times when the pain in our lives (or the life of someone we know and love) is so strong that it will cause tears. But God says that He will wipe away every tear from our eyes.

Our God can heal all hurts, you see. God can mend all wounds. God can make our life better. "I have come," Jesus said, "that you might have life and have it more abundantly" (John 10:10, paraphrased). In this new place there will be no more death. There will be no more mourning and crying. No more pain, for the old things have passed away. "I have come," God says, "to make all things new" (Revelation 21:5, paraphrased).

God's Agenda

A new world. A new society. A new community. A new way of thinking and speaking. The renewal starts with you, my sisters and brothers. It starts with you. It's not about a building. It's not about landscape. It's not about our surroundings or circumstances, although that's going to be a part of it. The change comes from God, but we must ask God to begin with us.

The only way we can have a new agenda—God's agenda— is to have a new heart, a new mind, and a new spirit. Think of it. If you come, God won't turn you away. God won't reject you. God takes us and makes us His own. God makes us new.

God's Word is trustworthy and true. God will be our God, and we will be God's people and God will dwell among us. As we are spiritually renewed, God works in and through us, completing His plan to make all things new.

BIBLE STUDY APPLICATION

Being Renewed

For a Christian, spiritual renewal is a way of life. It begins when we receive Christ as Lord and Saviour. But we do not become like Him instantly. We are constantly changing and growing to become the people that God wants us to be.

1. Use the following verses to describe God's role in the process of spiritual renewal.
     a) Philippians 1:6
     b) Philippians 2:13
     c) 1 Thessalonians 5:23-24
     d) 2 Timothy 1:9

    e) Hebrews 12:2
    f) 2 Peter 1:3

2. Use the following verses to describe how we are renewed.
    a) Psalm 51:10
    b) Isaiah 40:31
    c) Titus 3:5
    d) Ephesians 5:26-27; 1 Peter 1:23

3. Use the following verses to describe what part of us we are to renew.
    a) Psalm 51:10; Proverbs 20:8
    b) Ephesians 4:23
    c) 2 Corinthians 4:16; Colossians 3:10

4. Use the following verses to describe what part of us we are to offer to God as a spiritual sacrifice.
    a) Romans 12:2
    b) Hebrews 13:15
    c) Hebrews 13:16

Renewal in Process: Ambassadors for Christ

Now we are ambassadors for Christ and workers together with Him. Therefore, we encourage others to accept and receive the grace of God and the gift of salvation (2 Corinthians 5:20–6:2).

5. While on earth, we are God's work in process. Use the following verses to identify the purpose of spiritual renewal.
    a) 2 Corinthians 3:18; Romans 8:29
    b) 2 Peter 1:14
    c) 2 Corinthians 5:18-20

167

6. Use the following verses to identify the attributes of a
   renewed heart.
       a) Psalm 57:7
       b) Jeremiah 24:7
       c) Luke 8:15
       d) 2 Corinthians 4:6

7. Use the following verses to identify the benefits of a
   renewed mind.
       a) Romans 8:6
       b) 1 Corinthians 2:16; Philippians 2:5

8. Use the following verses to identify the requirements for
   spiritual vision.
       a) Matthew 5:8
       b) John 3:3
       c) John 16:14-15; 1 Corinthians 2:9-10
       d) Acts 26:18
       e) Colossians 1:26-27

Renewal Complete: Citizens of New Jerusalem

Before we believed in Christ, we were "aliens from the
commonwealth of Israel, and strangers from the covenants
of promise, having no hope, and without God in the world"
(Ephesians 2:12, NRSV). But, now we are no longer
"strangers and foreigners, but fellow-citizens with the
saints, and of the household of God" (Ephesians 2:19,
NRSV).

9. Use the verses in parentheses to answer the following
   questions.
       a) Who are we waiting for? (Colossians 3:4; 1 John
          3:2)
       b) What are we waiting for? (Romans 8:20-25)

c) What will we put on? (1 Corinthians 15:51-54)
d) Where is our citizenship? (Philippians 3:20-21)
e) What kind of city are we looking for? (Hebrews 11:10-16)
f) Describe our response. (Isaiah 65:17-19)
g) Whom will care for us? (Revelation 7:16-17)

10. Read Revelation 22:3-9. Use these verses to answer the following questions.
a) What shall be removed?
b) What shall be present?
c) What work will we do?
d) What will we see?
e) What will be the only source of light?
f) Will there be any darkness at all?
g) Whom should we worship?

PERSONAL APPLICATION

1. Read Philippians 2:12-13. Use these verses to describe the balance between God's work and our work in the process of our own spiritual renewal.

2. Your spiritual vision is affected by the time you regularly spend in prayer and in reading the Word of God. Is it time for a check-up?

3. We are partners in the work of God. Have you ever introduced someone to Christ?

4. Do you look forward to becoming a citizen of New Jerusalem? What do you think it will be like to live

without fear, pain, or death? What do you think it will
be like to live in the presence of God?

5. God's Word is trustworthy and true. How does the presence of the Holy Spirit in our lives assure us that the
vision will become reality? (Ephesians 1:14; 2
Corinthians 5:5)

CHURCH MINISTRY APPLICATION

1. How can the Church aid the process of spiritual renewal that takes place in every believer?

2. How can the Church help congregations keep the proper perspective on life?

3. How can the Church increase its outreach as ambassadors for Christ?

ENDNOTES

Chapter 1

[1] Howard Thurman, *Meditations of the Heart,* San Francisco: Howard Thurman Educational Trust, 1981, pp. 171-172, used by permission.

[2] Henry Mitchell, *Black Beliefs,* New York: Harper and Row Publishers, 1975, p. 139.

[3] Isaac Watts, *New National Baptist Hymnal,* Nashville: National Baptist Publishing Board, 1977, no. 135.

[4] Georgia Harkness, *Religious Living,* New York: Abingdon Press, 1937, pp. 48-51.

[5] Gayraud Wilmore, "Spiritual and Social Transformation as the Vocation of the Black Church," *Churches in Struggle,* New York, William K. Tabb (ed.), Monthly Review Press, 1986, p. 240.

Chapter 2

[6] Howard Thurman, *Meditations of the Heart,* San Francisco: Howard Thurman Educational Trust, 1981, pp. 215-216, used by permission.

Chapter 3

[7] Howard Thurman, *Meditations of the Heart,* San Francisco: Howard Thurman Educational Trust, 1981, used by permission.

Chapter 4

[8] James Melvin Washington, *Conversations With God,* New York: HarperCollins Publishers, Inc., 1994, p. 151.

[9] *Black Writers of America, A Comprehensive Anthology,* New York: Macmillan Publishing Co., 1972, pp. 869-870.

Chapter 5

[10] Howard Thurman, *Meditations of the Heart,* San Francisco: Howard Thurman Educational Trust, 1981, pp. 25-26, used by permission.

[11] Cleveland B. McAffe, *New National Baptist Hymnal,* Nashville: National Baptist Publishing Board, 1977, no. 426.

[12] Hugh Stowell, *Hymnal for Worship and Celebration,* Waco: Word Music Company, 1986, p. 432.

Chapter 6

[13] Howard Thurman, *Meditations of the Heart,* San Francisco: Howard Thurman Educational Trust, 1981, pp. 206-207, used by permission.

[14] Charles Albert Tindley, *New National Baptist Hymnal,* Nashville: National Baptist Publishing Board, 1977, no. 225.

[15] Howard Thurman, *Meditations of the Heart,* San Francisco: Howard Thurman Educational Trust, 1981, p. 206, used by permission.

[16] Myrna Summers, *God Gave Me a Song,* New York: Cotillion Records, Division of Atlantic Recording Company, 1970.

Chapter 7

[17] Howard Thurman, *Meditations of the Heart,* San Francisco: Howard Thurman Educational Trust, 1981, p. 183, used by permission.

Chapter 8

[18] Howard Thurman, *Meditations of the Heart,* San Francisco: Howard Thurman Educational Trust, 1981, pp. 46-47 ,used by permission.

Chapter 9

[19] Howard Thurman, *Meditations of the Heart,* San Francisco: Howard Thurman Educational Trust, 1981, pp. 196-197, used by permission.

Chapter 10

[20] Howard Thurman, *Meditations of the Heart,* San Francisco: Howard Thurman Educational Trust, 1981, p. 163, used by permission.

[21] Dietrich Bonhoeffer, *The Cost of Discipleship,* New York: Macmillan Publishing Company, 1963, p. 45.

Chapter 11

[22] James Melvin Washington, *Conversations With God,* New York: HarperCollins Publishers, Inc., 1994, p. 260.

Chapter 12

[23] James Melvin Washington, *Conversations With God,* New York: HarperCollins Publishers, Inc., 1994, p. 242.

BIBLIOGRAPHY

Bartlett, John. *Familiar Quotes.* Boston: Little, Brown, and Company, 1992.

Black Writers of America, A Comprehensive Anthology, New York: Macmillan Publishing Co., 1972.

Bonhoeffer, Dietrich. *The Cost of Discipleship.* New York: Macmillan Publishing Company, 1963.

Brown, Robert McAfee. *Spirituality and Liberation.* Philadelphia: Westminster Press, 1988.

Bruce, Calvin E. "Black Spirituality and Theological Method." *The Journal of the Interdenominational Theological Center,* vol. 3 (June 1986): 65-76.

_____. "Black Spirituality, Language and Faith." *Journal of Religious Education,* Yale Divinity School, vol. 71 (August 1976): 363-376.

Cone, James H. *Black Theology and Black Power.* New York: Seabury Press, 1969.

_____. *A Black Theology of Liberation* (1st edition). Philadelphia: Lippincott, 1970.

_____. "Black Worship." *The Study of Spirituality.* Cheslyn Jones, Geoffrey Wainwright, and Edward Yarnold (eds.). New York: Oxford University Press, 1986.

_____. *The Spirituals and the Blues: An Interpretation.* Westport: Greenwood Press, 1980.

173

Delaney, John J. (trans.). *The Practice of the Presence of God.* (Written by Brother Lawrence of the Resurrection.) Garden City: Image Books, 1977.

Hanson, Bradley (ed.). *Modern Christian Spirituality.* Atlanta: Scholars Press, 1990.

Harkness, Georgia. *Religious Living.* New York: Abingdon Press, 1937.

_____. *The Faith by Which the Church Lives.* New York: Abingdon Press, 1940.

_____. *Mysticism: Its Meaning and Message.* Nashville: Abingdon Press, 1973.

Jones, Major J. *The Color of God: The Concept of God in Afro-American Thought.* Macon: Mercer Press, 1987.

Lovell, John, Jr. *Black Song—The Forge and the Flame: The Story of How the Afro-American Spiritual Was Hammered Out.* New York: Macmillan Publishing Company, 1972.

Mbiti, John S. *African Religions and Philosophy.* Garden City: Doubleday, 1970.

_____. *Concepts of God in Africa.* New York: Praeger Publishers, 1970.

Merton, Thomas. *Contemplative Prayer.* New York: Herder and Herder, 1969.
_____. *Life and Holiness.* Garden City: Image Books, 1963.

Mitchell, Henry H. *Black Belief: Folk Beliefs of Blacks in America and West Africa* (1st edition). New York: Harper and Row Publishers, 1975.

New National Baptist Hymnal. Nashville: National Baptist Publishing Board, 1977.

Pannenberg, Wolfhart. *Christian Spirituality* (1st edition). Philadelphia: Westminster Press, 1983.

Sobrino, Jon (trans.). *Spirituality of Liberation: Toward Political Holiness.* Maryknoll: Orbis Books, 1988.

Stowell, Hugh. *Hymnal for Worship and Celebration.* Waco: Word Music Company, 1986.

Tabb, William K. (ed.). *Churches in Struggle: Liberation Theologies and Social Change in North America.* New York: Monthly Review Press, 1986.

Thurman, Howard. *Deep is the Hunger: Meditations for Apostles of Sensitiveness.* San Francisco: Howard Thurman Educational Trust.

_____. *Disciplines of the Spirit* (1st edition). San Francisco: Howard Thurman Educational Trust, 1981.

_____. *The Growing Edge.* San Francisco: Howard Thurman Educational Trust, 1981.

_____. *Meditations of the Heart.* San Francisco: Howard Thurman Educational Trust, 1981.

Trulear, Harold D. "The Lord Will Make a Way Somehow: Black Worship and the Afro-American Story." *The Journal of the Interdenominational Theological Center,* vol. 13 (Fall 1985): 87-106.

Underhill, Evelyn. *Mysticism* (12th edition, rev.). London: Methuen, 1930.

_____. *The Mystic Way: A Psychological Study in Christian Origins.* New York: E.P. Dutton, 1913.

_____. *The Spiritual Life.* New York: Harper and Row Publishers, 1936.

_____. *Worship.* New York: Harper and Row Publishers, 1937.

Washington, James Melvin. *Conversations With God.* New York: HarperCollins Publishers, Inc., 1994.

Wilmore, Gayraud S. *Black Religion and Black Radicalism: An Interpretation of the Religious History of Afro-American People.* Maryknoll: Orbis Books, 1983.

_____. "Spirituality and Social Transformation as the Vocation of the Black Church." *Churches in Struggle.* New York: Monthly Review Press, 1986.

Wilmore, Gayraud and James H. Cone (eds.). *Black Theology: A Documentary History 1966-1979.* Maryknoll: Orbis Books, 1979.